OXFORD SKILLS WORLD

Listening 2

WITH Speaking

Sarah Jane Lewis-Mantzaris

OXFORD
UNIVERSITY PRESS

OXFORD
UNIVERSITY PRESS

198 Madison Avenue
New York, NY 10016 USA

Great Clarendon Street, Oxford, OX2 6DP, United Kingdom

Oxford University Press is a department of the University of Oxford.
It furthers the University's objective of excellence in research, scholarship,
and education by publishing worldwide. Oxford is a registered trade
mark of Oxford University Press in the UK and in certain other countries

ISBN: 978 0 19 411336 6 STUDENT BOOK WITH WORKBOOK

Printed in China

This book is printed on paper from certified and well-managed sources

ACKNOWLEDGMENTS

Cover illustration and main character illustrations by: Shane McGowan/The
Organisation

Cover photograph: Sollina Images/Blend Images LLC/Getty

Back cover photograph: Oxford University Press building/David Fisher

Student Book

Illustrations by: Robin Boyer/Illustration Online pp.8–9, 22, 36, 37, 50, 53, 64, 78;
Pascale Constantin pp.30, 32, 82–83, 85; Monique Dong/Bright Group pp.67,
86; Kevin Fales/Maggie Byers Sprinzeles pp.26–27; John Kurtz pp.11, 43, 68,
81; Anthony Lewis/MB Artists pp.15–16, 23, 25, 46; Margeaux Lucas/MB Artists
pp.12–13; Steffane McClary/Maggie Byers Sprinzeles pp.40, 69, 71; Christos
Skaltsas/Advocate Art pp.18, 29, 54–55, 58, 88; Jomike Tejido/MB Artists pp.39,
55, 57, 72

*The Publishers would like to thank the following for their kind permission to reproduce
photographs and other copyright material*: 123rf: pp.8 (drawing/alchena), 10 (party
decorations/udra), 12 (classroom/federicofoto), 14 (1a/federicofoto), (4a/
Graham Oliver), 22 (run/tinna2727), (swing/Sabphoto), 24 (girl on swing/
bluerain22), 27 (children jumping rope/Iakov Filimonov), 28 (climbing/
Wavebreak Media Ltd), (children jumping rope/Iakov Filimonov), 40 (model
plane/Bogdan Ionescu), 42 (1a/Bogdan Ionescu), (1b/Audrius Merfeldas),
44 (dinosaur skeleton/James Kirkikis), (grand bazaar/Luciano Mortula),
52 (chef/Viaceslav Iakobchuk), (nurse/Luca Bertolli), 54 (barber/ferli), 56 (2b/
ferli), 64 (wash my face/Apatcha Muenaksorn), 66 (boy washing/Apatcha
Muenaksorn), 68 (evening/JIRAPONG BOONPONGHA), 70 (4a/JIRAPONG
BOONPONGHA), 78 (onion/Roman Stetsyk), (soup/Claudio Ventrella), 80 (boy
eating soup/Ukrid Yenpetch), 82 (milk/Monchai Tudsamalee), 84 (2b/Monchai
Tudsamalee); Alamy: pp.6–7 (floating school/Ana Flašker), 8 (stickers/Design
Pics Inc), 22 (jump/Radius Images), 24 (girl running/Wavebreak Media
ltd), (boy and girl walking/Radius Images), 28 (backetball/Image Source),
36 (t-shirt/Thanapol Kuptanisakorn), (vase/Khaled EdAdawy), 50 (zookeeper/
imageBROKER), 54 (postal worker/PHOTOINKE), 56 (1b/PHOTOINKE), (2a/
Wavebreak Media ltd), 60 (nurse outside hospital/Tony Tallec), 68 (afternoon/
Blend Images), 70 (1b/Blend Images), (4b/Blend Images), 80 (sandwich/liv
friis-larsen/Alamy Stock Photo), (cabbage/Anjo Kan); Getty: pp.8 (classmates/
ERproductions Ltd), 12 (coat hooks/Erik Isakson), 14 (2b/Lisa Stirling), (3b/
Erik Isakson), 24 (boy jumping/stray_cat), 26 (hobby/Marc Romanelli),
(sports/Sorapong Chaipanya/EyeEm), 28 (soccer/Lorado), (girl painting/
Marc Romanelli), 34–35 (flower stall/Alys Tomlinson), 41 (clothing store/
Blend Images-Erik Isakson), 51 (different professions/Yuri Arcurs), 52 (artist/
Blend Images), 54 (librarian/Andersen Ross), 56 (1a/Andersen Ross), 64 (get
dressed/Image Source), (walk to school/David De Lossy), 66 (walking to
school/fstop.123), 68 (day/Christoph Hetzmannseder), 70 (3b/Christoph
Hetzmannseder), 76–77 (family eating dinner/BJI/Blue Jean Images);

Oxford University Press: pp.20–21 (children zorbing/Shutterstock/Jorg
Hackemann), 26 (hop/Oxford University Press Australia), 28 (hopscotch/
Oxford University Press Australia), 36 (smartphone/Shutterstock/Umberto
Shtanzman), 40 (camera/Shutterstock; neelsky), (shopping cart/Shutterstock/
Levent Konuk), 42 (3b/Shutterstock/Michelangelus), (4a/Shutterstock/
Levent Konuk), (4b/Shutterstock/neelsky), 50 (nurse/Shutterstock/Monkey
Business Images), 64 (morning/Shutterstock/Lapse studio), 70 (2b/Galyna
Andrushko/Shutterstock), 82 (potato/Shutterstock/Deep OV), 84 (2a/Oxford
University Press ANZ/Brent Parker Jones), (3b/Shutterstock/Deep OV), (4b/Mike
Stone); Shutterstock: pp.8 (decorations/Cora Mueller), 10 (boys in artclass/
mangpor2004), (drawing of rainbow/volkovslava), (stickers/Dmytro Yashchuk),
12 (globe/titov dmitriy), 14 (1b/wavebreakmedia), (3a/titov dmitriy), (walk/
Tayawee Supan), 26 (rollerblade/Sergey Novikov), 27 (children rollerblading/
Sergey Novikov), 28 (rollerblade/Sergey Novikov), (sports montage/artproem),
36 (clothes on hanger/Africa Studio), 38 (folded t-shirts/xiaorui), (vases/Nataly
Reinch), (woman clothes shopping/frantic00), (girl with smartphone/Ljupco
Smokovski), 40 (toy dinosaur/Zubaru), 41 (indoor market/khanongjansri),
42 (2a/Luisa Leal Photography), (2b/Zubaru), (3a/Pavel L Photo and Video),
44 (fruit market/James Wagstaff), 48–49 (wildlife photographer/Volodymyr
Burdiak), 50 (chef/wavebreakmedia), (painter/Photographee.eu), 51 (adult
class/Monkey Business Images), 52 (zookeeper/Elena Kirey), 54 (server/
Palplaner), 56 (3a/Palplaner), (3b/riat), (4a/Golden Pixels LLC), (4b/George
Rudy), 62–63 (world clock/Nattee Chalermtiragool), 65 (girl using laptop in the
dark/vinnstock), (girl using laptop in the light/Ronnachai Palas), 66 (breakfast/
wavebreakmedia), (getting dressed/Ronnachai Palas), 68 (sleep/Hung Chung
Chih), 70 (1a/275847), (2a/Littlekidmoment), (3a/Hung Chung Chih), 74 (boy
on cellphone/Sabphoto), 78 (cabbage/beats1), (chicken/MShev), 79 (children
eating lunch/SpeedKingz), (children cooking/Iakov Filimonov), 80 (onions/
Bukhta Yurii), 82 (sausage/zoryanchik), (sweetcorn/Polina Prokofieva), 84 (1a/
zoryanchik), (1b/Polina Prokofieva), (3a/Joe Gough), (4a/koss13)

Workbook

Illustrations by: Robin Boyer/Illustration Online pp.99, 111; Kevin Fales/
Maggie Byers Sprinzeles pp.93, 107; John Kurtz p.91; Anthony Lewis/MB
Artists pp.101, 113; Steffane McClary/Maggie Byers Sprinzeles p.109; Christos
Skaltsas/Advocate Art pp.97, 105; Jomike Tejido/MB Artists p.95

*The Publishers would like to thank the following for their kind permission to reproduce
photographs and other copyright material*: 123rf: pp.92 (1b/alchena), (3a/udra),
94 (1b/Graham Oliver), (3c/federicofoto), 96 (1a/tinna2727), (1b/bluerain22),
98 (1a/Wavebreak Media Ltd), (2c/Iakov Filimonov), 102 (1a/Audrius Merfeldas),
(1b/Bogdan Ionescu), (2b/Bogdan Ionescu), 103 (2/Cathy Yeulet), 104 (1a/
Viacheslav Iakobchuk), (4a/ferli), 106 (1a/ferli), 108 (1b/Apatcha Muenaksorn),
(2b/Apatcha Muenaksorn), 110 (2/JIRAPONG BOONPONGHA), 112 (1a/
Claudio Ventrella), (2b/Roman Stetsyk), (3a/Ukrid Yenpetch), 114 (1b/Monchai
Tudsamalee); Alamy: 92 (3b/Design Pics Inc/Alamy Stock Photo), 96 (2a/
Wavebreak Media ltd/Alamy Stock Photo), (2b/Radius Images), (4a/Radius
Images), 98 (2b/Image Source/Alamy Stock Photo), 100 (2a/Khaled EdAdawy/
Alamy Stock Photo), (3a/Thanapol Kuptanisakorn), 104 (3b/imageBROKER/
Alamy Stock Photo), 106 (2c/Wavebreak Media ltd/Alamy Stock Photo), (3c/
PHOTOINKE/Alamy Stock Photo), 110 (1a/liv friis-larsen/Alamy Stock Photo),
(3c/Blend Images), 112 (2a/Anjo Kan), (4b/liv friis-larsen/Alamy Stock Photo);
Getty: 92 (2a/ERproductions Ltd), 94 (1a/Erik Isakson), (2b/Lisa Stirling), 96 (3b/
stray_cat), 98 (1c/Lorado), (3b/Marc Romanelli), 104 (3a/Blend Images), 106 (1b/
Andersen Ross), (3b/Andersen Ross), 108 (2a/Image Source), (3a/David De
Lossy), (4a/fstop.123), 110 (2b/Christoph Hetzmannseder); Oxford University
Press: 98 (1b/Oxford University Press Australia), 100 (1b/Shutterstock; Umberto
Shtanzman), 102 (1c/Shutterstock; Michelangelus), (2a/Shutterstock; neelsky),
(2c/Shutterstock/Levent Konuk), 104 (1b/Shutterstock; Monkey Business
Images), 106 (1c/Chris King), 108 (4b/Shutterstock/Lapse studio), 110 (2a/
Shutterstock/Lapse studio), 114 (1a/Oxford University Press ANZ/Brent
Parker Jones), (2a/Shutterstock/Deep OV), (2c/Mike Stone), (3b/Mike Stone);
Shutterstock: 92 (1a/Dmytro Yashchuk), (2b/volkovslava), (4a/Cora Mueller),
(4b/mangpor2004), 94 (2c/titov dmitriy), (3a/wavebreakmedia), 96 (3a/Tayawee
Supan), (4b/Cheryl Ann Quigley), 98 (2a/Sergey Novikov), (3a/artproem), (3c/
Sergey Novikov), 100 (1a/Africa Studio), (2b/xiaorui), (3b/Ljupco Smokovski),
(4a/Nataly Reinch), (4b/frantic00), 102 (3a/Pavel L Photo and Video), (3b/
Luisa Leal Photography), (3c/Zubaru), 103 (1/Farknot Architect), 104 (2a/
Elena Kirey), (2b/Photographee.eu), (4b/wavebreakmedia), 106 (2a/Palplaner),
(2b/riat), (3a/Golden Pixels LLC), 108 (1a/wavebreakmedia), (3b/Ronnachai
Palas), 110 (1b/275847), (1c/Hung Chung Chih), (3a/Ronnachai Palas), (3b/
Littlekidmoment), 112 (1b/Bukhta Yurii), (3b/MShev), (4a/beats1), 114 (1c/Joe
Gough), (2b/Polina Prokofieva), (3a/koss13), (3c/zoryanchik)

Table of Contents

Hi! I'm Olly.

Hi, I'm Molly!

Introduction

Welcome to Oxford Skills World

Oxford Skills World: Listening with Speaking is a flexible paired skills course that takes students on a journey toward independent learning, providing them with strategies and support to reach their goals.

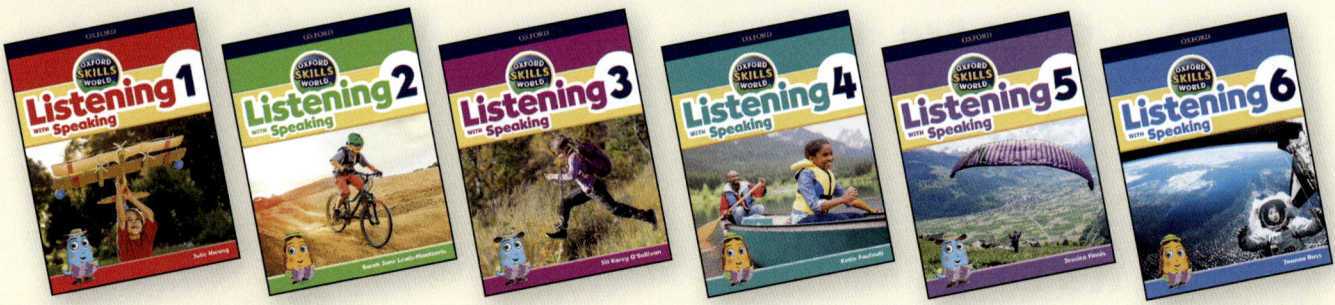

For Students

- Student Book / Workbook
- Student's website with downloadable audio and extra resources
  www.oup.com/elt/oxfordskillsworld

For Teachers

- Downloadable Teacher's Pack with instructional support, assessment, professional development videos, projects, and speaking resources
- Classroom Presentation Tool
- Teacher's website with downloadable audio and extra resources
  www.oup.com/elt/teacher/oxfordskillsworld

Be the Leader on Your Skills Adventure!

Hi! We're Olly and Molly, your skills adventure guides. We help you reach your goals by introducing new listening and speaking strategies, asking helpful questions, and giving friendly reminders. Most importantly, we cheer you on every step of the way! Let's go!

Quick Guide

Inside Each Topic

Topic Opener

Theme-based topics provide high-interest content relevant to students' lives.

My Goals introduces students to the objectives of each unit in the topic.*

Students listen to a Fun Fact to increase their engagement with the topic.

Fun characters, Olly and Molly, encourage 21st century skills like critical thinking, collaboration, and communication.

Students answer questions to activate prior knowledge and think critically.

Get Ready to Listen • Listen

Students learn and practice new vocabulary and complete the picture dictionary at the back of the book.

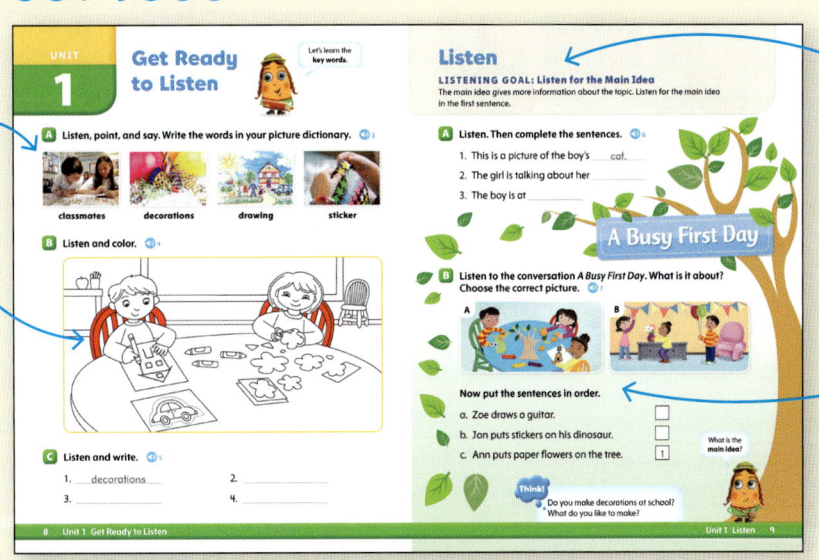

Listening Goals are strategies students can apply to any passage.

Students apply strategies to high-interest fiction and nonfiction passages, think critically about what they hear, and make connections to their own lives.

*Each topic contains two thematically related units.

Quick Guide

Understand

Students increase their comprehension of the passages by applying listening strategies they have learned.

Students complete activities to strengthen their understanding of the unit's vocabulary.

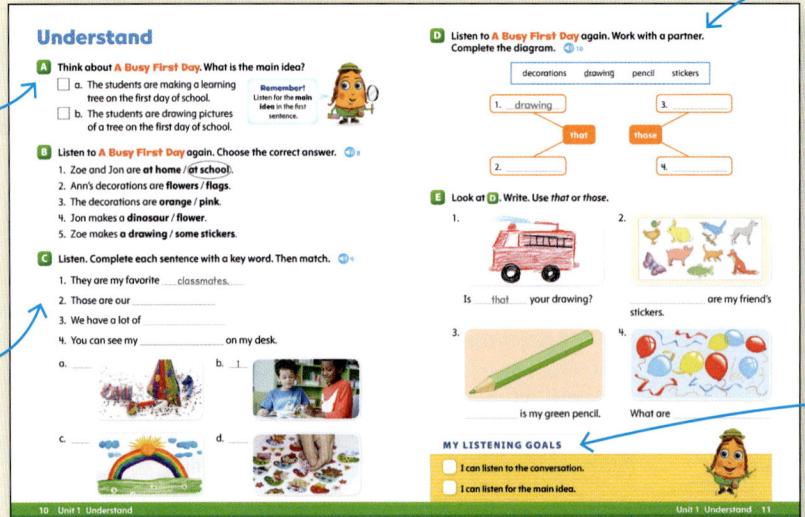

Students demonstrate comprehension of the unit's passage, vocabulary, and grammar.

At the end of each unit, students assess the progress they have made toward achieving their goals.

Listening Check

With helpful reminders from Olly and Molly, students apply the **Listening Goals** from both units to a new text.

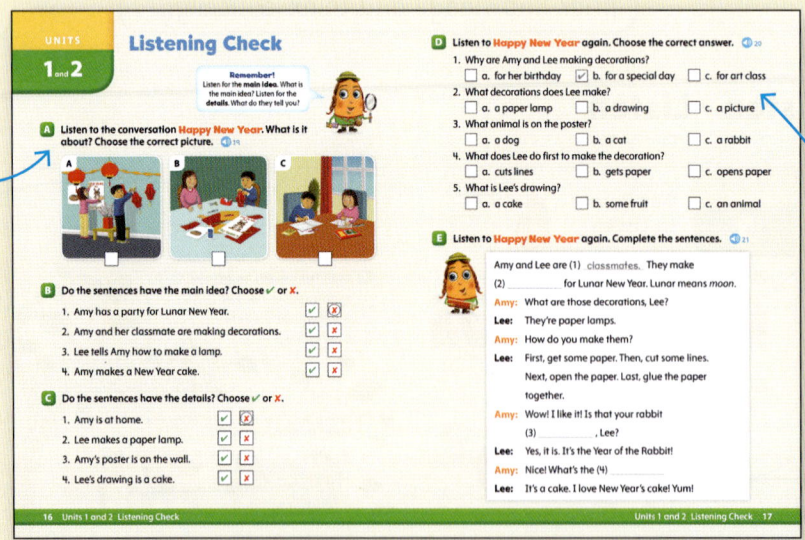

Students complete activities to boost listening comprehension and vocabulary application.

Get Ready to Speak • Speak

Speaking Goals prepare students to speak in different contexts.

Speaking Tips provide guidance on grammar, punctuation, and mechanics and help students speak fluently and accurately.

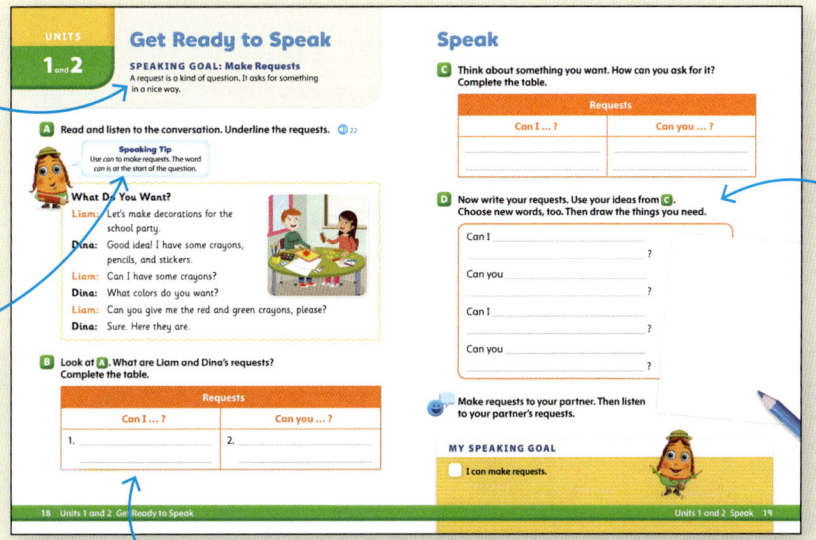

Students use graphic organizers to comprehend speaking models and to organize their thoughts for their own speaking.

Scaffolded speaking models help students accomplish their speaking goals.

Workbook

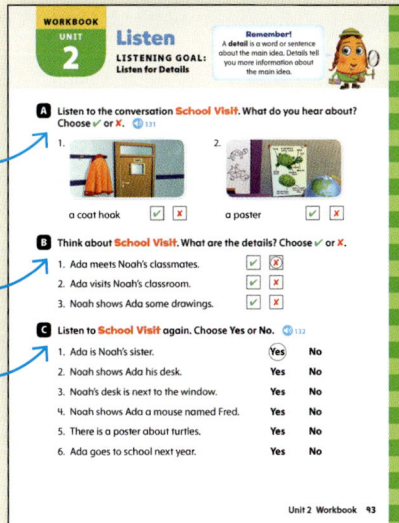

Workbook pages at the end of the book provide more opportunities for students to apply their **Listening Goals** and boost comprehension.

Additional activities provide extra opportunities for listening comprehension and vocabulary practice.

Students apply the topic's **Speaking Tip** to ensure proper usage in their own speaking.

School Life

MY GOALS

UNIT 1

- Listen to the conversation *A Busy First Day*
- Listen for the main idea

UNIT 2

- Listen to the story *Guess What?*
- Listen for details

SPEAK

- Make requests

A Look at the picture. What do you see?

1. Where are the children? What are they doing?

2. Is your classroom like this? Why or why not?

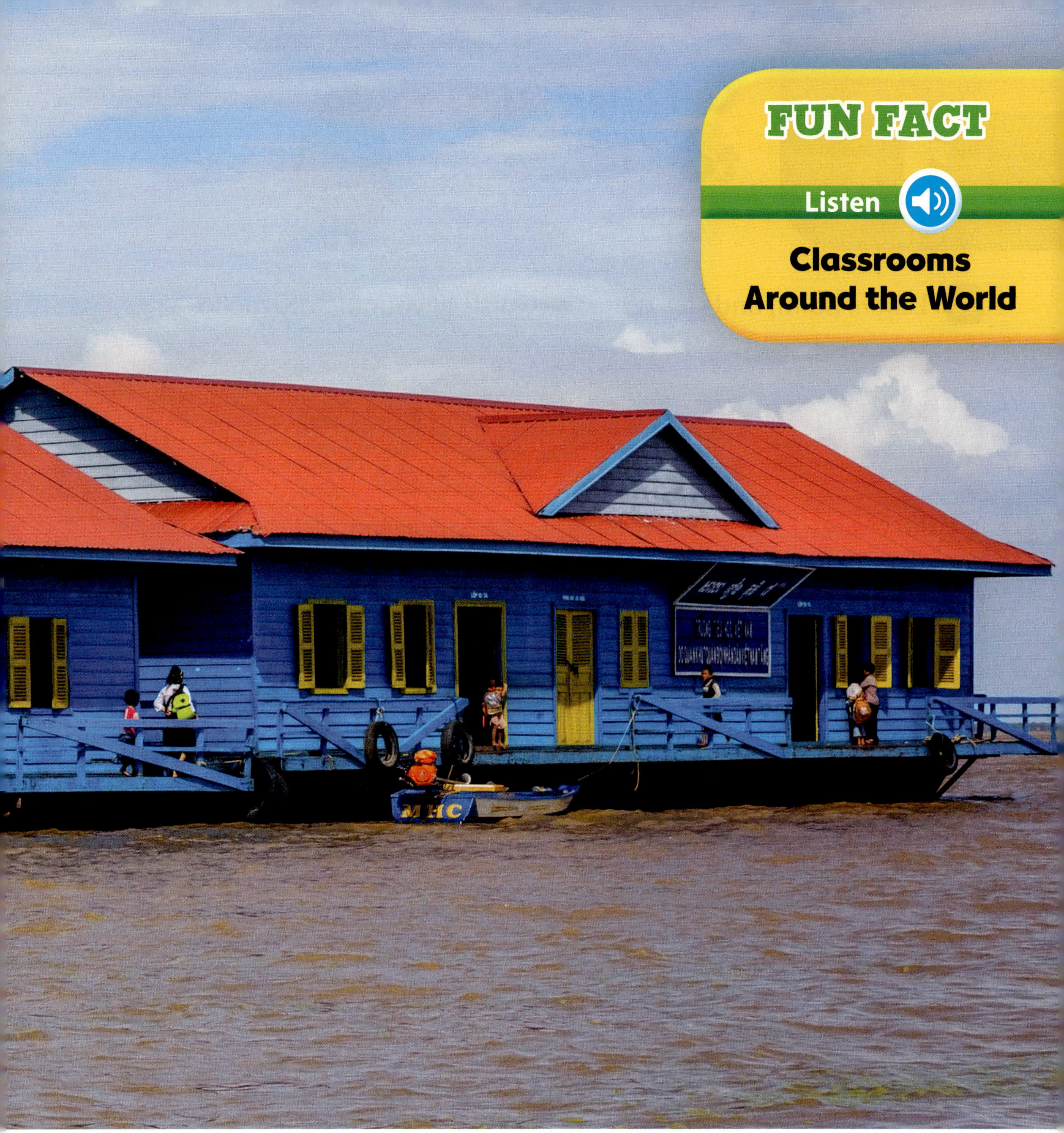

FUN FACT

Listen

Classrooms Around the World

B **Listen to the Fun Fact. Then answer the questions.** 2

1. Where is the school?
2. What do you like about the school? Why?

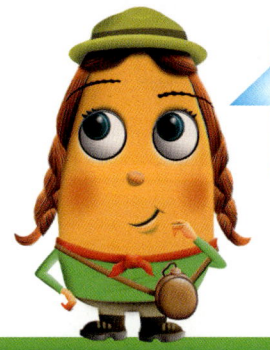

Think, Pair, Share
What is your favorite thing about your school? Why?

Get Ready to Listen

Let's learn the **key words.**

A Listen, point, and say. Write the words in your picture dictionary. 3

classmates

decorations

drawing

sticker

B Listen and color. 4

C Listen and write. 5

1. ___decorations___   2. _____

3. _____   4. _____

Listen

The main idea gives more information about the topic. Listen for the main idea in the first sentence.

A Listen. Then complete the sentences.  6

1. This is a picture of the boy's ____cat.____

2. The girl is talking about her _____

3. The boy is at _____

A Busy First Day

B Listen to the conversation *A Busy First Day*. What is it about? Choose the correct picture.  7

A

B

Now put the sentences in order.

a. Zoe draws a guitar. ☐

b. Jon puts stickers on his dinosaur. ☐

c. Ann puts paper flowers on the tree. 1

What is the **main idea**?

Think!

Do you make decorations at school? What do you like to make?

Understand

A Think about **A Busy First Day**. What is the main idea?

☐ a. The students are making a learning tree on the first day of school.

☐ b. The students are drawing pictures of a tree on the first day of school.

> **Remember!**
> Listen for the **main idea** in the first sentence.

B Listen to **A Busy First Day** again. Choose the correct answer. 🔊 8

1. Zoe and Jon are **at home** / (at school).
2. Ann's decorations are **flowers** / **flags**.
3. The decorations are **orange** / **pink**.
4. Jon makes a **dinosaur** / **flower**.
5. Zoe makes **a drawing** / **some stickers**.

C Listen. Complete each sentence with a key word. Then match. 🔊 9

1. They are my favorite ____classmates.____

2. Those are our _____

3. We have a lot of _____

4. You can see my _____ on my desk.

a. ____

b. __1__

c. ____

d. ____

D Listen to **A Busy First Day** again. Work with a partner. Complete the diagram. 🔊 10

decorations   ~~drawing~~   pencil   stickers

1. drawing

that

2. _____

3. _____

those

4. _____

E Look at **D**. Write. Use *that* or *those*.

1.

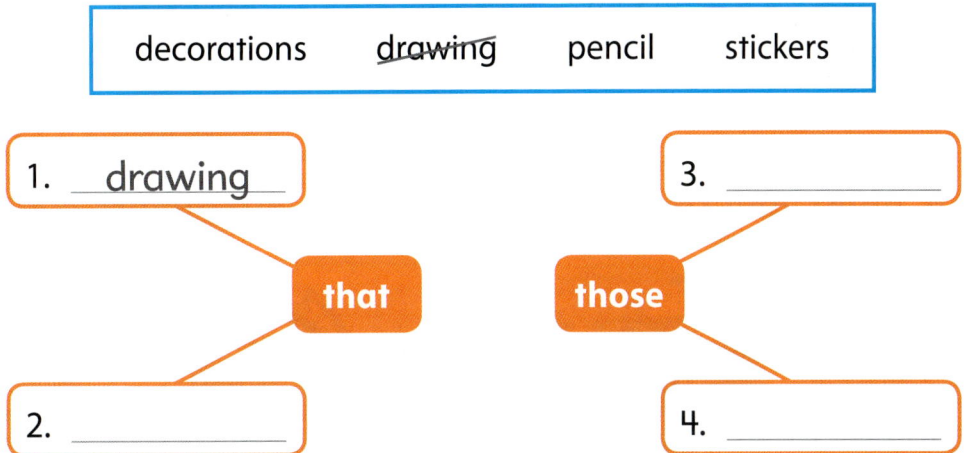

Is ____that____ your drawing?

2.

_____ are my friend's stickers.

3.

_____ is my green pencil.

4.

What are _____

MY LISTENING GOALS

☐ I can listen to the conversation.

☐ I can listen for the main idea.

Get Ready to Listen

Let's learn the **key words**.

A Listen, point, and say. Write the words in your picture dictionary. 11

classroom

coat hooks

globe

poster

B Listen and number. 12

C Listen and complete the sentences. 🔊 13

1. They are making a ___poster___ for the wall.

2. My teacher has a _____ on her desk.

3. Our _____ is very big.

4. My _____ is next to the door.

Listen

LISTENING GOAL: Listen for Details

A detail is a word or a sentence about the main idea. Listen for details to learn more information about the main idea.

A Listen. Choose ✔ or ✘. 14

1.
2.
3.

 ✘   ✘   ✘

Guess What?

B Listen to the story *Guess What?* Choose the correct picture. 15

A

B

Now choose ✔ or ✘.

1. Two people talk in the story. ✔ ⊗

2. They talk about school. ✔ ✘

3. The students are playing a game. ✔ ✘

What are the **details**?

Think!
• Do you play games at school? Tell your partner.

Understand

A **Think about Guess What?**
Are these details? Choose Yes or No.

1. There is a poster in the classroom. **Yes** **No**

2. The children are playing a game. **Yes** **No**

B **Listen to Guess What? again. Choose the correct answer.** 🔊 16

1. When do the children play the game?

   ☐ a. the beginning of class ☑ b. the end of class

2. The teacher says *big and round*. The students think it is

   ☐ a. a ball. ☐ b. a globe.

3. What is on the wall?

   ☐ a. a poster ☐ b. a drawing

C **Listen and choose the correct picture. Then write the key word.** 🔊 17

1.

   ☑ a. ☐ b.

   _____classroom_____

2.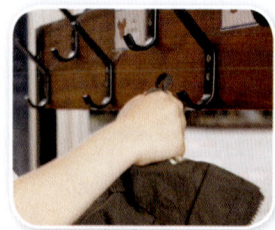

   ☐ a. ☐ b.

3.

   ☐ a. ☐ b.

4.

   ☐ a. ☐ b.

Is it / Are they … ?		Yes, it is. / Yes, they are.
1. ____Is it a globe?____	→	____Yes, it is.____
2. _____ coat hooks?	→	_____
3. _____ a poster?	→	_____
4. _____ a classroom?	→	_____

E Look at **D**. Write. Use *Is it* or *Are they* for the questions.

1.

____Is it____ a globe?

____Yes, it is.____

2.

_____ coat hooks?

_____

3.

_____ a poster?

_____

4.

_____ a classroom?

_____

MY LISTENING GOALS

☐ I can listen to the story.

☐ I can listen for details.

Listening Check

> **Remember!**
> Listen for the **main idea**. What is the main idea? Listen for the **details**. What do they tell you?

A Listen to the conversation **Happy New Year**. What is it about? Choose the correct picture. 🔊 19

A

B

C

B Do the sentences have the main idea? Choose ✔ or ✘.

1. Amy has a party for Lunar New Year. ✔ ⊗
2. Amy and her classmate are making decorations. ✔ ✘
3. Lee tells Amy how to make a lamp. ✔ ✘
4. Amy makes a New Year cake. ✔ ✘

C Do the sentences have the details? Choose ✔ or ✘.

1. Amy is at home. ✔ ⊗
2. Lee makes a paper lamp. ✔ ✘
3. Amy's poster is on the wall. ✔ ✘
4. Lee's drawing is a cake. ✔ ✘

Listen to Happy New Year again. Choose the correct answer. 🔊 20

1. Why are Amy and Lee making decorations?
   ☐ a. for her birthday   ☑ b. for a special day   ☐ c. for art class

2. What decorations does Lee make?
   ☐ a. a paper lamp   ☐ b. a drawing   ☐ c. a picture

3. What animal is on the poster?
   ☐ a. a dog   ☐ b. a cat   ☐ c. a rabbit

4. What does Lee do first to make the decoration?
   ☐ a. cuts lines   ☐ b. gets paper   ☐ c. opens paper

5. What is Lee's drawing?
   ☐ a. a cake   ☐ b. some fruit   ☐ c. an animal

E **Listen to Happy New Year again. Complete the sentences.** 🔊 21

Amy and Lee are (1) _classmates._ They make

(2) _____ for Lunar New Year. Lunar means *moon*.

Amy: What are those decorations, Lee?

Lee: They're paper lamps.

Amy: How do you make them?

Lee: First, get some paper. Then, cut some lines.

Next, open the paper. Last, glue the paper

together.

Amy: Wow! I like it! Is that your rabbit

(3) _____, Lee?

Lee: Yes, it is. It's the Year of the Rabbit!

Amy: Nice! What's the (4) _____

Lee: It's a cake. I love New Year's cake! Yum!

Get Ready to Speak

SPEAKING GOAL: Make Requests

A request is a kind of question. It asks for something in a nice way.

A Read and listen to the conversation. Underline the requests. 22

Speaking Tip
Use *can* to make requests. The word *can* is at the start of the question.

What Do You Want?

Liam: Let's make decorations for the school party.

Dina: Good idea! I have some crayons, pencils, and stickers.

Liam: Can I have some crayons?

Dina: What colors do you want?

Liam: Can you give me the red and green crayons, please?

Dina: Sure. Here they are.

B Look at **A**. What are Liam and Dina's requests? Complete the table.

Requests	
Can I … ?	**Can you … ?**
1. _____ _____	2. _____ _____

Speak

C Think about something you want. How can you ask for it? Complete the table.

Requests	
Can I ... ?	**Can you ... ?**
_____ _____	_____ _____

D Now write your requests. Use your ideas from **C**. Choose new words, too. Then draw the things you need.

Can I _____
_____ ?

Can you _____
_____ ?

Can I _____
_____ ?

Can you _____
_____ ?

 Make requests to your partner. Then listen to your partner's requests.

MY SPEAKING GOAL

☐ I can make requests.

Games Are Fun!

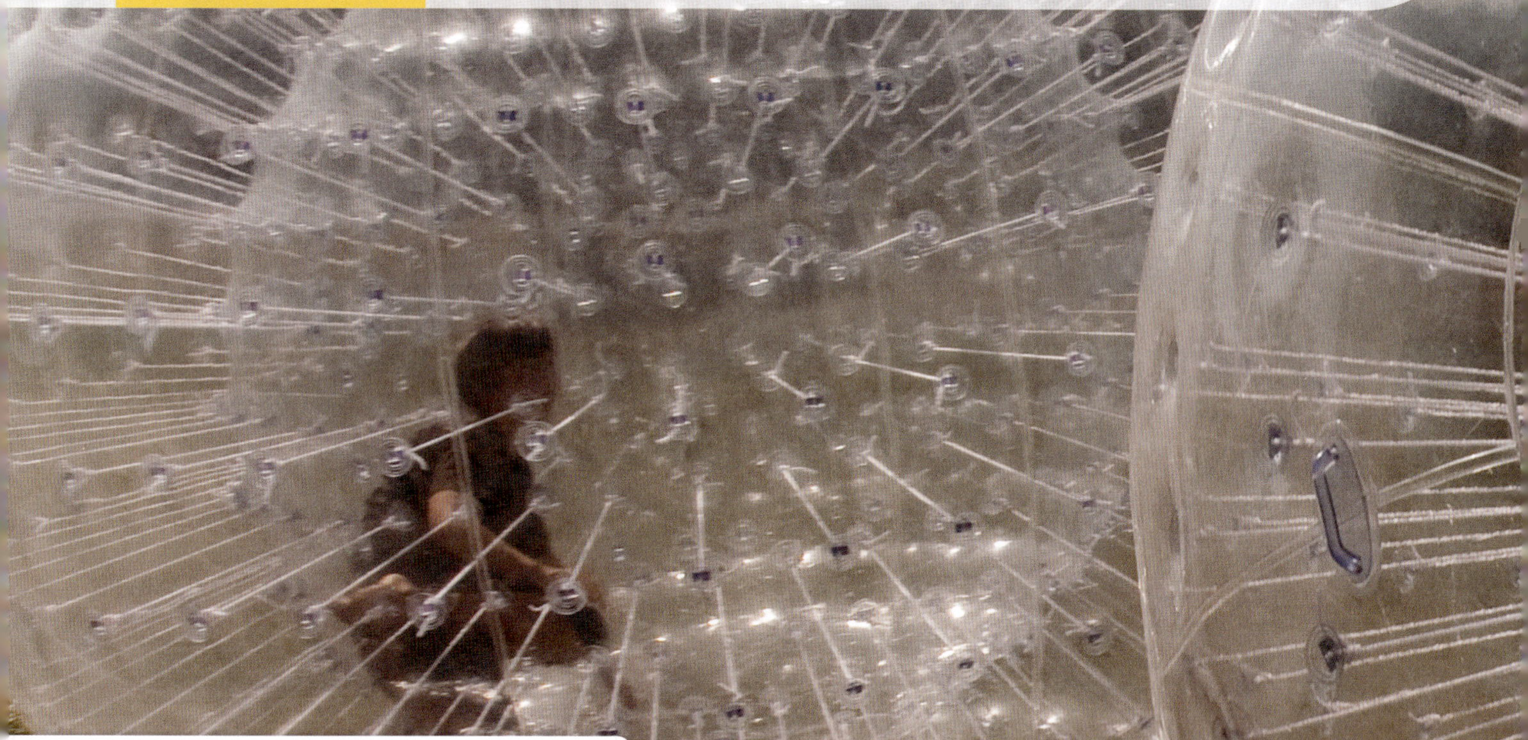

MY GOALS

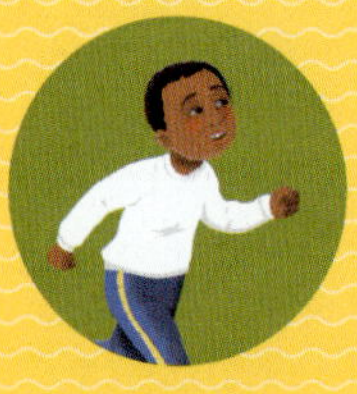

UNIT 3

- Listen to the story *A Time for Sports*
- Listen for action words

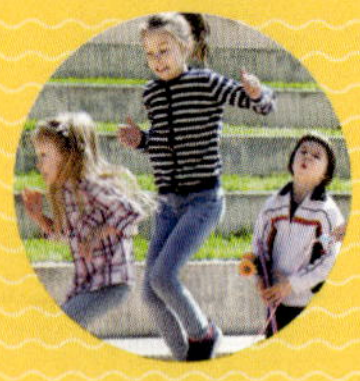

UNIT 4

- Listen to the passage *A Fun Hobby*
- Listen for gist

SPEAK

- Describe routines

A Look at the picture. What do you see?

1. Where are the children?

2. Where do you play games like this? When?

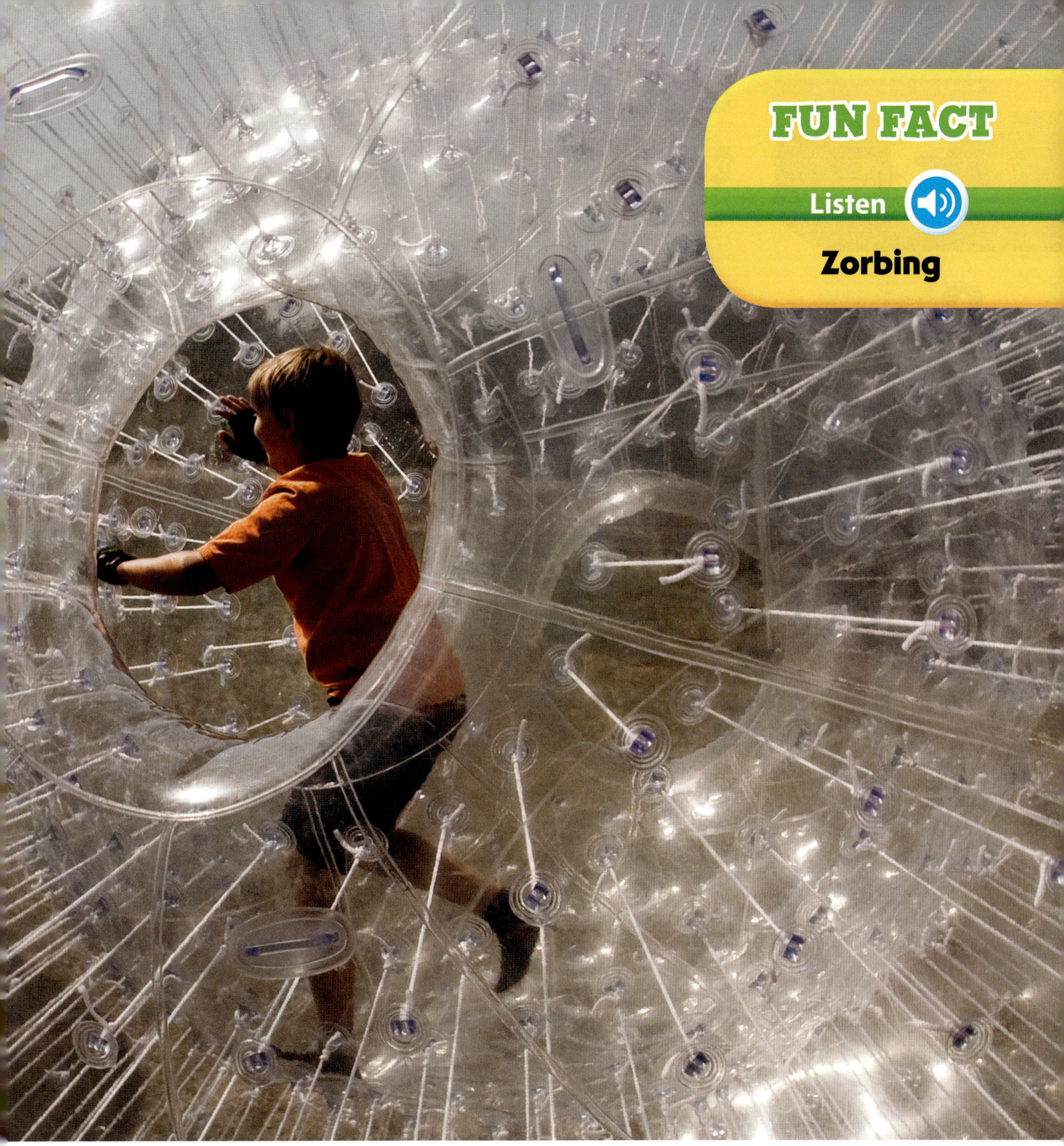

FUN FACT

Listen

Zorbing

B **Listen to the Fun Fact. Then answer the questions.** 23

1. How does zorbing work?
2. Do you want to try zorbing? Why or why not?

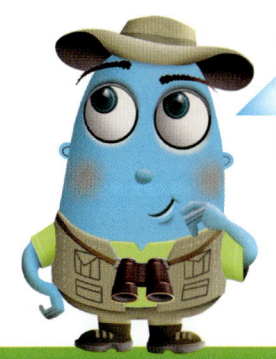

Think, Pair, Share
What games do you play?

Get Ready to Listen

Let's learn the **key words**.

A Listen, point, and say. Write the words in your picture dictionary. 24

jump

run

swing

walk

B Listen and color. 🔊 25

C Listen and write. 🔊 26

1. _____swing_____

2. _____

3. _____

4. _____

Listen

LISTENING GOAL: Listen for Action Words

Words like *run*, *jump*, and *swing* are action words. Listen for action words to know what the people in a story are doing.

A　**Listen. Then complete the sentences.** 🔊 27

1. Kim plays soccer and ___runs___ with the ball.

2. Pedro _____ to school with his friends.

3. Sue _____ into the water with her sister.

A Time for Sports

B　**Listen to the story *A Time for Sports*. What is it about? Choose the correct picture.** 🔊 28

A

B

Now put the sentences in order.

a. Adam and Beth see a man running.　☐

b. Adam shows Beth the games.　1

c. They see a man jumping.　☐

What is the most important idea?

Think! Do you like watching games or playing games? Why?

Understand

A Think about **A Time for Sports**.
What actions do the people do?

- ☐ a. They run, jump, and swing.
- ☐ b. They walk, swim, and skip.

B Listen to **A Time for Sports** again. Choose the correct answer. 🔊 29

1. Beth and Adam are watching people play (games)/ **soccer**.
2. Beth and Adam see a **man** / **woman** first.
3. The man can **walk** / **run** really fast.
4. Next, Beth and Adam see the man **run** / **jump.**
5. Beth **can** / **can't** swing.

C Listen. Complete each sentence with a key word. Then match. 🔊 30

1. They ____walk____ to school.

2. She _____ in the park.

3. Don't _____ in class!

4. Ceci can _____ high.

a. ____

b. ____

c. ____

d. __1__

D Listen to **A Time for Sports** again. What can the people do? Work with a partner. Complete the diagram.  31

1. _Can she_ see?

2. _____ run?

Can he / she / they … ?

3. _____ jump?

4. _____ swing?

E Look at **D**. Write. Use *Can he, Can she,* or *Can they.*

1.

_____Can she see?_____

Yes, she can.

2.

_____

Yes, they can.

3.

_____

Yes, he can.

4.

_____

No, she can't.

MY LISTENING GOALS

☐ I can listen to the story.

☐ I can listen for action words to know what people in the story are doing.

Get Ready to Listen

Let's learn the **key words**.

A Listen, point, and say. Write the words in your picture dictionary. 32

hobby

hop

rollerblade

sports

B Listen and number.  33

C Listen and complete the sentences.  34

1. My brother and I can ___hop___ fast.

2. We _____ at the park on Saturday.

3. I have a fun _____

4. We play many _____ at school.

Listen

LISTENING GOAL: Listen for Gist

The gist is what a listening passage is mostly about. To know the gist, listen for names, action words, and places. Also, look at the pictures, title, and activity questions.

A Listen. Choose ✔ or ✘. 🔊 35

1.

2.

3.

B Listen to the passage *A Fun Hobby*. What is it about? Choose the correct picture. 🔊 36

A Fun Hobby

A

B

Now choose ✔ or ✘.

1. Jade rollerblades in many ways. ✔ ✘

2. Jade is learning to rollerblade. ✔ ✘

3. The passage is about school. ✔ ✘

How can you know the **gist** of the passage?

Think!

Do you have a fun hobby? What is it? What do you like about it?

Understand

A **Think about A Fun Hobby. What is the gist? Choose Yes or No.**

1. Jade only likes to rollerblade
at the park with her friends. **Yes** **No**

2. Jade rollerblades in many
ways and in many places. **Yes** **No**

> **Remember!**
> Listen for **gist** to find out what a passage is mostly about.

B **Listen to A Fun Hobby again. Choose the correct answer.** 🔊 37

1. How does Jade rollerblade?
   - [ ] a. She can run.
   - [✔] b. She can jump.

2. Why does Jade rollerblade to school?
   - [ ] a. It's fast.
   - [ ] b. She can race.

3. Why does Jade like to rollerblade?
   - [ ] a. She likes to make new friends.
   - [ ] b. It's fun and good for her.

C **Listen and choose the correct picture. Then write the key word.** 🔊 38

1. [✔] a.   [ ] b.

   rollerblade

2. [ ] a.   [ ] b.

3. [ ] a.   [ ] b.

4. [ ] a.   [ ] b.

D Listen to **A Fun Hobby** again. What does Jade like? What doesn't she like? Work with a partner. Complete the diagram. 🔊 39

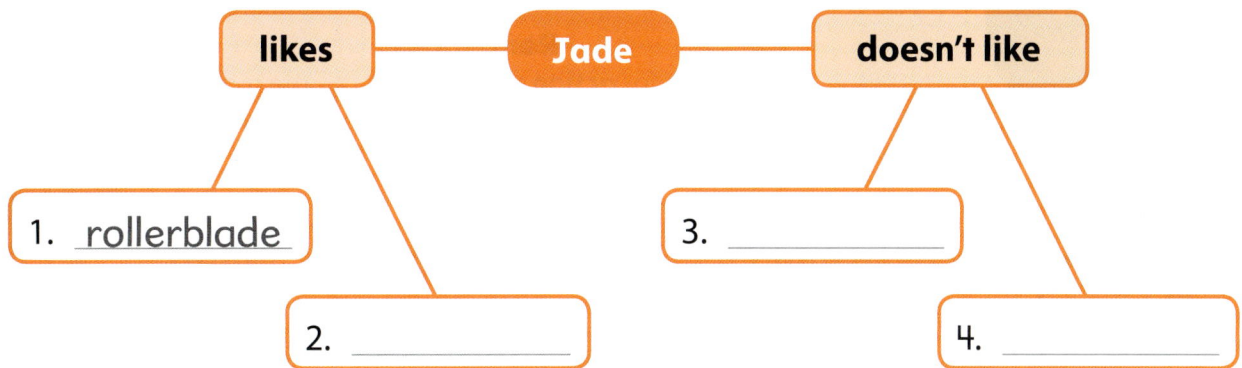

| likes | Jade | doesn't like |

1. _rollerblade_

2. _____

3. _____

4. _____

E Look at **D**. Write. Use *Yes, she does* or *No, she doesn't.*

1.

Does Jade like to rollerblade?

_____ Yes, she does. _____

2.

Does Jade like to walk?

_____

3.

Does Jade like to go fast?

_____

4.

Does Jade like to go slow?

_____

MY LISTENING GOALS

☐ I can listen to the passage.

☐ I can listen for the gist of the passage.

Listening Check

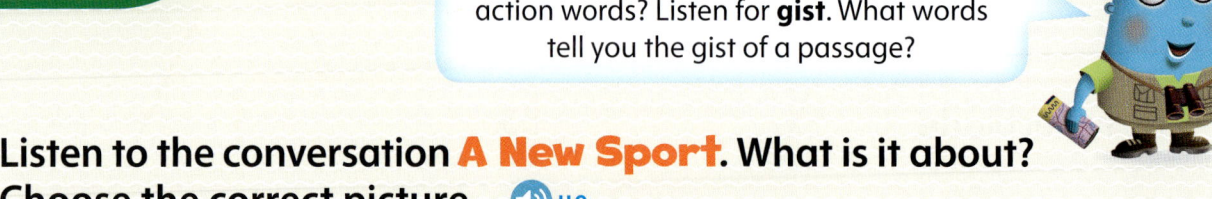

A Listen to the conversation **A New Sport**. What is it about? Choose the correct picture. 🔊 40

A

B

C

B Which sentences have action words? Choose ✔ or ✘.

1. I run fast. ✔ ✘

2. I don't like basketball. ✔ ✘

3. I jump high. ✔ ✘

4. It's fun! ✔ ✘

C What is the gist of the conversation? Choose ✔ or ✘.

1. Luke plays soccer and tennis. ✔ ✘

2. Luke wants to try a new sport. ✔ ✘

3. Tony and Luke make a new friend. ✔ ✘

4. Luke and Tony are friends. ✔ ✘

Listen to A New Sport again. Choose the correct answer. 🔊 41

1. What day does Luke play tennis?
   ☐ a. Monday   ☐ b. Wednesday   ☑ c. Friday

2. Who does Luke talk to?
   ☐ a. his brother   ☐ b. his friend   ☐ c. a teacher

3. What can Luke do?
   ☐ a. hop   ☐ b. rollerblade   ☐ c. jump high

4. What sport doesn't Luke like?
   ☐ a. basketball   ☐ b. soccer   ☐ c. tennis

5. What can Jade do?
   ☐ a. jump   ☐ b. rollerblade   ☐ c. dance

E **Listen to A New Sport again. Complete the sentences.** 🔊 42

Luke plays (1) ___sports___ at school. He plays soccer on Tuesday and tennis on Friday. Now he wants to try a new sport. He talks to his friend, Tony.

Luke: Let's try a new sport, Tony.

Tony: OK! What can you do?

Luke: I (2) _____ fast. I (3) _____ high.

Tony: Hm. Do you like basketball?

Luke: No, I don't.

Tony: Hey, Jade! We want to try a new sport. What can you do?

Jade: I can (4) _____ fast!

Tony: Let's try to rollerblade!

Luke: OK! Let's do it!

Get Ready to Speak

SPEAKING GOAL: Describe Routines
Routines are the things you do often. Routines describe what you do and when.

A Read and listen to the routine. Underline the time phrases. 43

Speaking Tip
Use time phrases like *every Monday*, *Wednesday to Friday*, and *on the weekend* to show when.

**My Weekly Routine
by Jane**

I do karate every Monday. From Wednesday to Friday, I run in the mornings. But I don't play sports on the weekend. I walk in the park with my friends. And I ride my bike. I sleep a lot, too.

B Look at **A**. What is Jane's routine? Complete the diagram.

My Weekly Routine

1. Monday	2. Wednesday to Friday	3. Weekend
do karate	_____	_____
_____	_____	_____

Speak

C Think about sports you play or hobbies you do. What is your routine?

My Weekly Routine

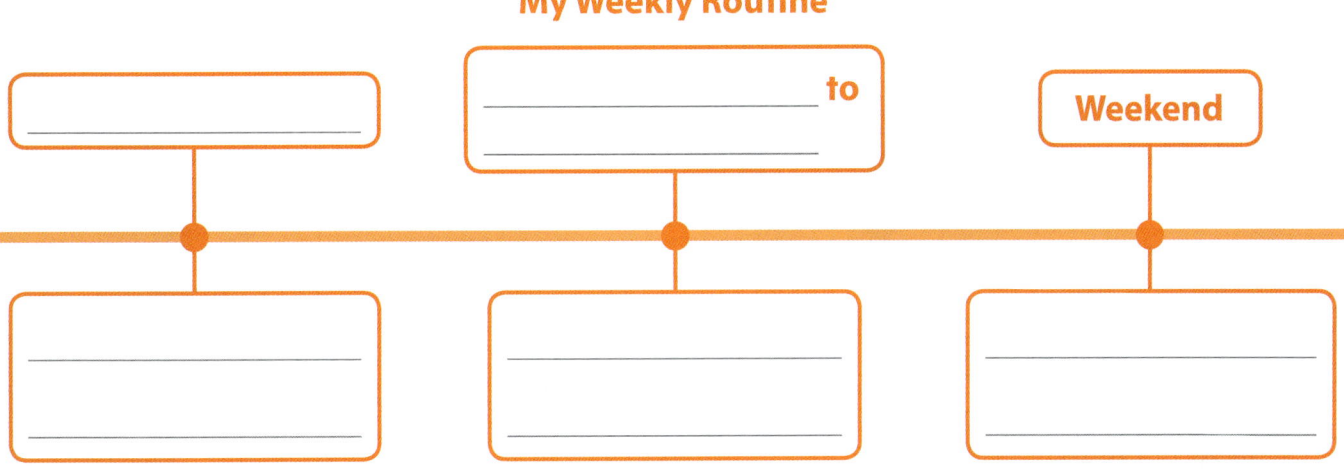

D Now write your routine. Use your ideas from **C**. Choose new words, too. Then draw yourself playing your sport or doing your hobby.

On _____, _____
_____.

From _____ to _____,
_____.

On the weekend, _____
_____.

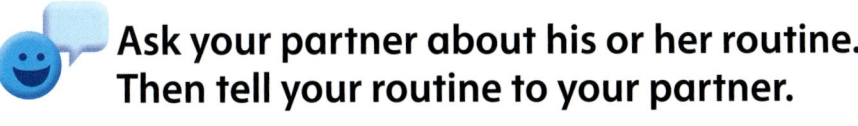 Ask your partner about his or her routine. Then tell your routine to your partner.

MY SPEAKING GOAL

☐ I can describe a routine.

TOPIC 3

It's Shopping Time!

MATH

MY GOALS

UNIT 5

- Listen to the story *A Gift for Mom*
- Listen for prices

UNIT 6

- Listen to the announcement *Megamarket*
- Listen for days of the week

SPEAK

- Exchange information

 A **Look at the picture. What do you see?**

1. Where is the woman? What is she doing?

2. Where does your family go shopping?

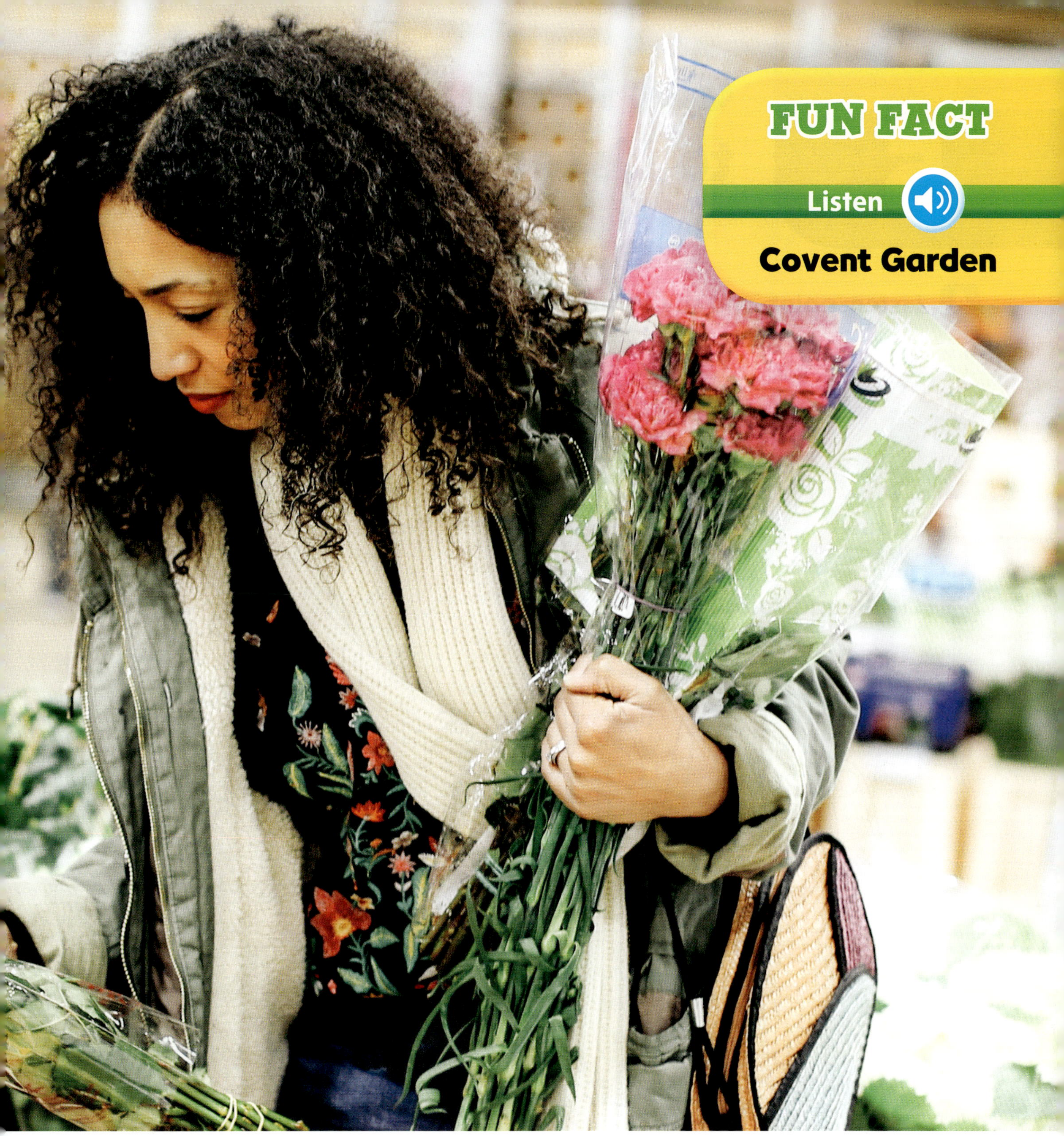

FUN FACT

Listen

Covent Garden

B **Listen to the Fun Fact. Then answer the questions.** 44

1. What kind of place is it?
2. Do you want to go there? Why or why not?

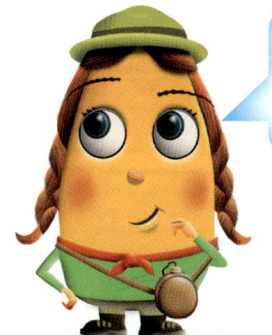

Think, Pair, Share
What things do you like to buy?

Get Ready to Listen

Let's learn the **key words**.

A **Listen, point, and say. Write the words in your picture dictionary.** 45

clothes

smartphone

T-shirt

vase

B **Listen and color.** 46

C **Listen and write.** 47

1. _____clothes_____

2. _____

3. _____

4. _____

Listen

A Listen. Choose the correct answer. 🔊 48

1. ✔ a. 20 dollars ☐ b. 30 dollars
2. ☐ a. 12 dollars ☐ b. 10 dollars
3. ☐ a. 90 cents ☐ b. 19 cents

A Gift for Mom

B Listen to the story *A Gift for Mom*. What is it about?
Choose the correct picture. 🔊 49

A ☐

B ☐

Now put the sentences in order.

a. Tara shows the salesclerk a picture of her mom. ☐

b. Tara can buy the small vase. ☐

c. Tara talks to the salesclerk. 1

What **prices** do you hear?

Think!
How do you pay for things in a store? What do you do when you don't have enough money?

Understand

Remember!
Price words, like *dollars* and *cents*, tell you how much something is.

A Think about **A Gift for Mom**.
What do the price words tell you?

☐ a. They tell you how much the vases are.

☐ b. They tell you how much the T-shirts are.

B Listen to **A Gift for Mom** again. Choose the correct answer. 🔊 50

1. Tara is at a **mall** / (**market**).

2. Tara is with her **mom** / **father**.

3. Tara's mom has red **hair** / **clothes**.

4. Tara has 10 **cents** / **dollars**.

5. Tara buys a **small** / **large** vase.

C Listen. Complete each sentence with a key word. Then match. 🔊 51

1. My mom likes ___clothes.___

2. This is my new _____

3. My mom doesn't like _____

4. There are _____ in the market.

a. ____

b. ____

c. __1__

d. ____

D Listen to **A Gift for Mom** again. Complete the diagram. 🔊 52

Does she have / like … ?	Yes	No
1. clothes	✔	
2. red hair		
3. nice shirt		
4. vase		

E Look at **D**. Write. Use *Yes, she does* or *No, she doesn't*.

1.

Does she like clothes?

_____Yes, she does._____

2.

Does she have red hair?

_____

3.

Does she have a nice shirt?

_____

4.

Does she have a vase?

_____

MY LISTENING GOALS

☐ I can listen to the story.

☐ I can listen for prices to find out how much something is.

Get Ready to Listen

Let's learn the **key words**.

A Listen, point, and say. Write the words in your picture dictionary. 🔊 53

camera

plane

shopping cart

toy

B Listen and number. 🔊 54

C Listen and complete the sentences. 🔊 55

1. There are a lot of ____toys____ in the store.

2. That _____ is dirty.

3. My brother's _____ is black.

4. Tom has a small _____

Listen

LISTENING GOAL: Listen for Days of the Week
Words like *Monday* and *Wednesday* are days of the week. Listen for days to know when something happens.

A Listen and complete the sentences.  56

1. The toy store isn't open on ___Sunday.___

2. The boy's birthday is on _____

3. The girl has an art class on _____

Megamarket

B Listen to the announcement *Megamarket*. What is it about? Choose the correct picture.  57

A

B

Now choose ✔ or ✗.

1. The man says it's Monday.   ✅ ✗

2. Cameras are four dollars.   ✔ ✗

3. The man talks about clothes.   ✔ ✗

> What **days** does the man say in the announcement?

Think!
Do you hear announcements at stores?
What do the announcements say?

Understand

A Think about **Megamarket**. What days do you hear?
Choose **Yes** or **No**.

1. Monday   **Yes**   **No**
2. Thursday   **Yes**   **No**

> **Remember!**
> **Days** tell you when
> something happens.

B Listen to **Megamarket** again. Choose the correct answer. 🔊 58

1. What day can you buy planes for five dollars?
   ☑ a. Tuesday   ☐ b. Friday
2. What day can you eat ice cream?
   ☐ a. on Sundays   ☐ b. on Saturday
3. How much is the ice cream?
   ☐ a. 25 cents   ☐ b. 99 cents

C Listen and choose the correct picture. Then write the key word. 🔊 59

1.
☑ a.   ☐ b.

_____ plane _____

2.
☐ a.   ☐ b.

3.
☐ a.   ☐ b.

4.
☐ a.   ☐ b.

_____   _____

D Listen to **Megamarket** again. Where are the things? Work with a partner. Complete the table. 🔊 60

1. cameras → <u>camera store</u>

2. planes → _____

3. paint → _____

4. ice cream → _____

E Look at **D**. Write. Use *It's* or *They're*.

1.

Where are the cameras?

<u>They're in the camera store.</u>

2.

Where are the planes?

_____

3.

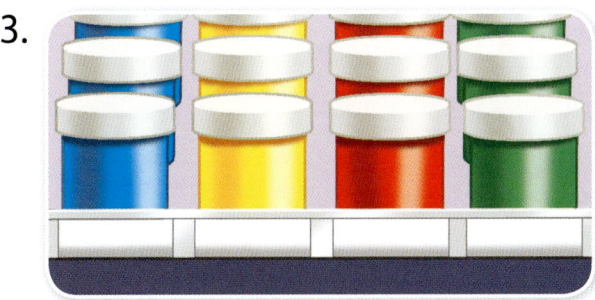

Where is the paint?

_____

4.

Where is the ice cream?

_____

MY LISTENING GOALS

☐ I can listen to the announcement.

☐ I can listen for days of the week.

Listening Check

Remember!
Listen for numbers and **price words**.
What are the prices? Listen for **days of the week**. What do they tell you?

A Listen to the passage **The Grand Bazaar**.
What is it about? Choose the correct picture. 🔊 61

A

B

C

B Are the prices correct? Choose ✔ or ✘.

1. The T-shirt is 5 dollars. ✔ ✘

2. The T-shirt is 50 dollars. ✔ ✘

3. The candy is 50 cents. ✔ ✘

4. The candy is 15 cents. ✔ ✘

C Are the days correct? Choose ✔ or ✘.

1. They go to the market on Saturday. ✔ ✘

2. They go to the market on Tuesday. ✔ ✘

3. Their friend's birthday is on Sunday. ✔ ✘

4. Their friend's birthday is on Monday. ✔ ✘

Listen to The Grand Bazaar again. Choose the correct answer. 🔊 62

1. What is the Grand Bazaar?

   ☐ a. a mall   ☑ b. a market   ☐ c. a store

2. Who does Ian go to the Grand Bazaar with?

   ☐ a. his brother   ☐ b. his dad   ☐ c. his friend

3. What do they want to buy at the market?

   ☐ a. a gift   ☐ b. toys   ☐ c. paint

4. What does Ata buy?

   ☐ a. a smartphone   ☐ b. some candy   ☐ c. a T-shirt

5. What does Ian buy?

   ☐ a. a T-shirt   ☐ b. some candy   ☐ c. a plane

E **Listen to The Grand Bazaar again. Complete the sentences.** 🔊 63

The Grand Bazaar is in Turkey. It's an old market with a lot of stores. I go with my friend, Ata. Ata knows all the places! We go on Saturday. It's our friend's birthday on Sunday. We want to buy a birthday gift for our friend here. I like (1) ___toys___. Ata likes (2) _____. Ata buys a (3) _____. It's five dollars. I buy some (4) _____. It's 50 cents! Now, what can we buy for our friend? It's fun to go shopping at the Grand Bazaar!

Get Ready to Speak

SPEAKING GOAL: Share Information

We tell the things we know. We ask about the things we want to know.

A Read and listen to the information. Underline the phrases that ask for more information.  64

> **Speaking Tip**
> Use questions like *What about you?* to learn information about someone.

What about you?

Tom: What's your favorite store?

Kim: It's the toy store. I can buy scooters there.

Tom: Nice!

Kim: What about you? What's your favorite store?

Tom: I like the clothes store. I can buy T-shirts there.

B Look at **A**. What do Tom and Kim say? Complete the table.

	Favorite Store	Things to Buy
Kim		
Tom		

Speak

C Think about your favorite store. What can you buy there?
Complete the table.

Favorite Store	Things to Buy

D Now write. Share information. Use your ideas from **C**.
Then draw something from the store.

What's your favorite store?

It's the _____ store.

I can _____

_____.

What about you?
What's your favorite store?

It's the _____ store.

I can _____

_____.

 Ask your partner about his or her
favorite store. Then tell your partner
about your favorite store.

MY SPEAKING GOAL

☐ I can exchange information.

Where Do People Work?

MY GOALS

UNIT 7

- Listen to the interview *Working Around the World*
- Listen for places

UNIT 8

- Listen to the conversation *New Friends*
- Listen for addresses

SPEAK

- Describe a place

A Look at the picture. What do you see?

1. Where is the man? What is he doing?
2. Do people do this in your country? Why or why not?

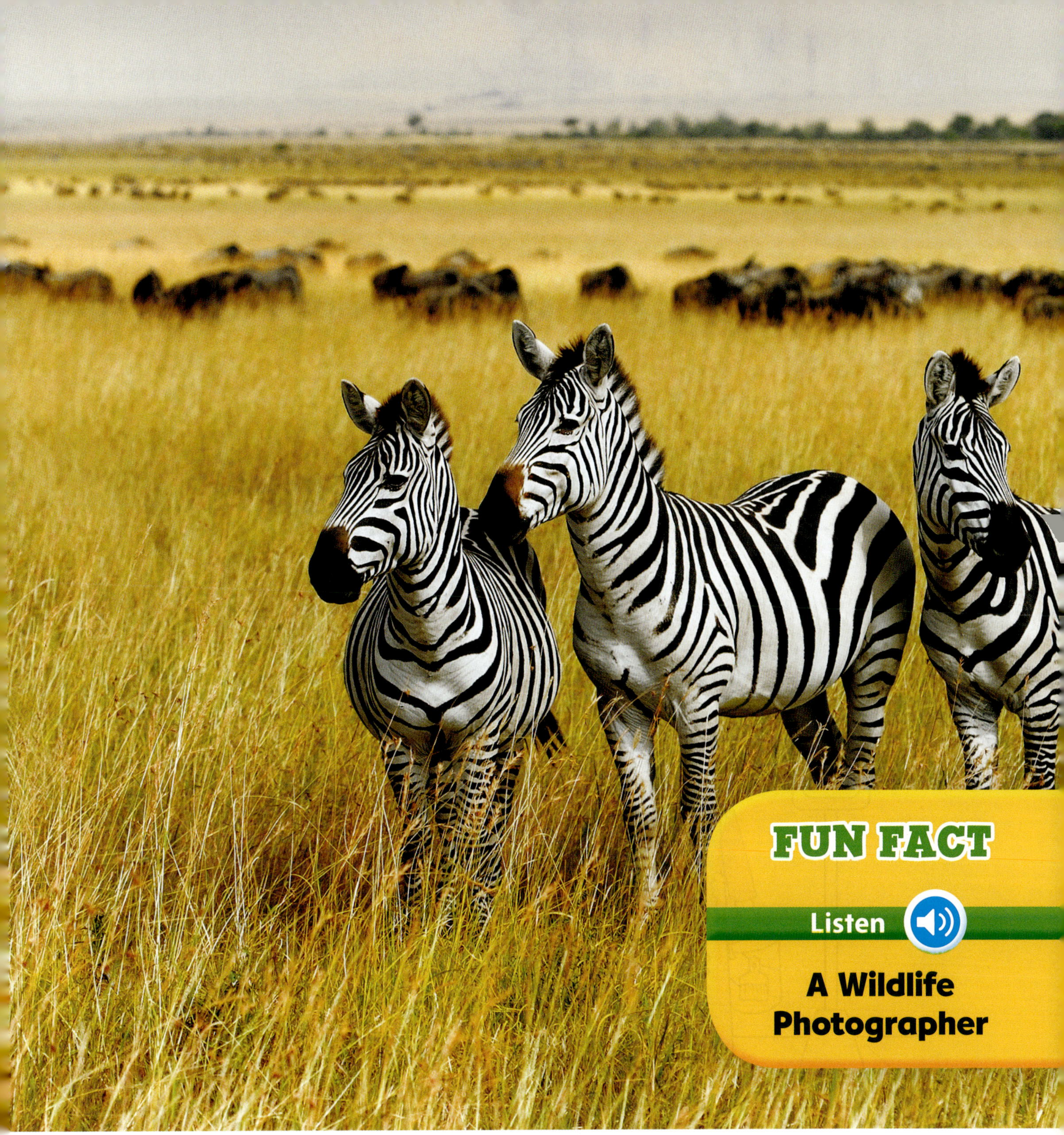

FUN FACT

Listen

A Wildlife Photographer

B **Listen to the Fun Fact. Then answer the questions.** 65

1. What is the man's job?
2. Do you like this kind of job? Why or why not?

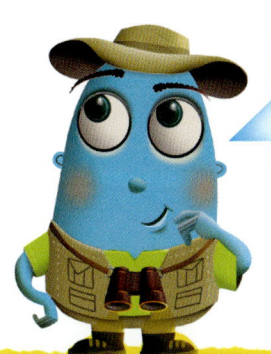

Think, Pair, Share
What job do you want to do? Why?

Get Ready to Listen

Let's learn the **key words**.

A Listen, point, and say. Write the words in your picture dictionary. 66

chef

nurse

painter

zookeeper

B Listen and color. 67

C Listen and write. 68

1. ____zookeeper____

2. _____

3. _____

4. _____

Listen

LISTENING GOAL: Listen for Places

Places are countries, cities, and buildings. *Turkey*, *Seoul*, and *a school* are places.
Listen to places to know where people are.

A   Listen. What is the place? Choose the correct answer. 🔊 69

1. ☐ a. a school   ✔ b. a home
2. ☐ a. a city   ☐ b. a building
3. ☐ a. a country   ☐ b. a city

Working Around the World

B   Listen to the interview *Working Around the World*.
What is it about? Choose the correct picture. 🔊 70

A   ☐

B   ☐

Now put the sentences in order.

a. Tam talks to a chef.   ☐

b. Tam meets Mary and Bill.   1

c. Tam speaks to a zookeeper.   ☐

> Where are the people?
> What jobs do they do?

Think!
> What other jobs do you know?
> Where do the people work?

Understand

A Think about **Working Around the World**. What places are in the interview?

☐ a. Mexico   ☐ b. a restaurant
☐ c. a school   ☐ d. China

B Listen to **Working Around the World** again. Choose the correct answer. 🔊 71

1. Mary helps sick **animals** / (**people**).
2. Bill paints **houses** / **pictures**.
3. Raúl works as a **chef** / **teacher**.
4. Meg is a **zookeeper** / **nurse**.
5. Meg works with **people** / **animals**.

C Listen. Complete each sentence with a key word. Then match. 🔊 72

1. This is my mom. She's a ___painter.___
2. My uncle is a _____. I go see him at work.
3. This is my dad. He's a _____
4. Aunt Emma is a _____. She's nice.

a. ____

b. ____

c. ____

d. __1__

Listen to **Working Around the World** again. Work with a partner. Complete the table. 🔊 73

Mary	Who _is she?_	_She's_ a nurse.
Bill and Tom	Who _____	_____ painters.
Raúl	Who _____	_____ a chef.
Meg	Who _____	_____ a zookeeper.

E Look at D. Write. Use *is* or *are*.

1.

Who _____ is she? _____

_____ She's a nurse. _____

2.

Who _____

_____

3.

Who _____

_____

4.

Who _____

_____

MY LISTENING GOALS

☐ I can listen to the passage.

☐ I can listen for places to know where people are.

Get Ready to Listen

Let's learn the **key words**.

A Listen, point, and say. Write the words in your picture dictionary. 74

barber

librarian

postal worker

server

B Listen and number. 75

C Listen and complete the sentences. 🔊 76

1. My sister is a ___server.___

2. The _____ is in the van.

3. The _____ is at her desk.

4. My dad is a _____ in the city.

Listen

An address has a number and street name. It shows where a building is.
Listen for addresses to know where people live or work.

A **Listen and number.** 🔊 77

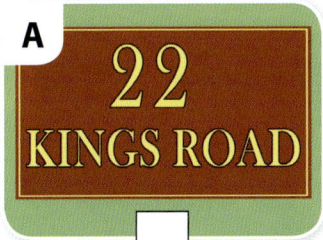
A

B

C

1

New Friends

B **Listen to the conversation *New Friends*. What is it about? Choose the correct picture.** 🔊 78

A

B

Now choose ✔ or ✘.

1. The boys talk about people at their school. ✔ ⊗

2. Lee tells Han where people work. ✔ ✘

3. Han wants to know where the barber works. ✔ ✘

What do the **addresses** tell you?

Think! Do you have these people in your city? Where do they work?

Understand

A Think about **New Friends**.
Choose **Yes** or **No**.

Remember!
An **address** has a number and street name. It shows where people live or work.

1. Brian works at 65 Elm Street.   **Yes**   **No**
2. Mr. Kim works at 22 Oak Street.   **Yes**   **No**

B Listen to **New Friends** again. Choose the correct answer. 79

1. Who do Han and Lee talk about first?
   - ✔ a. a librarian
   - ☐ b. a postal worker

2. Who works at Maple Restaurant?
   - ☐ a. Jack
   - ☐ b. Brian

3. What does Mr. Kim do?
   - ☐ a. He's a server.
   - ☐ b. He's a barber.

C Listen and choose the correct picture. Then write the key word. 80

1.

   ☐ a.   ✔ b.

   _____postal worker_____

2.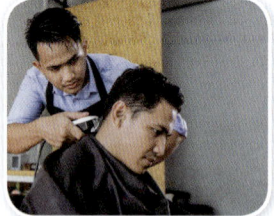

   ☐ a.   ☐ b.

   _____

3.

   ☐ a.   ☐ b.

   _____

4.

   ☐ a.   ☐ b.

   _____

D Listen to **New Friends** again. Complete the diagram.  81

What does he / she do?   **Where does he / she work?**

1. _____librarian_____ → library

2. _____ → post office

3. _____ → restaurant

4. _____ → barber shop

E Look at **D**. Write. Use *What* or *Where*.

1.

___Where___ does she work?

She works in a library.

2.

_____ does he do?

He's a postal worker.

3.

_____ does he work?

He works in a restaurant.

4.

_____ does he do?

He's a barber.

MY LISTENING GOALS

☐ I can listen to the conversation.

☐ I can listen to addresses to know where people live or work.

Listening Check

Remember!
Listen for **places**. Where are the people? Listen for **addresses**. Where do they live or work?

A Listen to the conversation **The Guessing Game**. What is it about? Choose the correct picture. 🔊 82

B Do the sentences have places? Choose ✔ or ✘.

1. Ellie and Max are at home. ✔ ✘

2. They work at 24 Park Street. ✔ ✘

3. Max lives at 45 Main Street. ✔ ✘

4. Max's mom works in a restaurant. ✔ ✘

C Do the sentences have addresses? Choose ✔ or ✘.

1. Ellie and Max play a game at home. ✔ ✘

2. The servers work at 24 Park Street. ✔ ✘

3. Max lives at 45 Main Street. ✔ ✘

4. Max's mom is a librarian. ✔ ✘

D Listen to **The Guessing Game** again. Choose the correct answer. 🔊 83

1. What job does Max guess first?
   ☐ a. server   ☑ b. barber   ☐ c. postal worker

2. Who works at 24 Park Street?
   ☐ a. barbers   ☐ b. postal workers ☐ c. servers

3. What is the number of Max's house?
   ☐ a. 44   ☐ b. 45   ☐ c. 46

4. Who is a postal worker?
   ☐ a. Max's dad   ☐ b. Max's mom   ☐ c. Ellie's dad

5. Where does Max's mom work?
   ☐ a. at a restaurant ☐ b. at a library   ☐ c. at a post office

E Listen to **The Guessing Game** again. Complete the sentences. 🔊 84

Ellie and Max play a game at home.

Ellie: Ready? Let's play! They work at 24 Park Street.

Who are they?

Max: Hmm. (1) _Barbers?_

Ellie: No. They work in a restaurant.

Max: Are they (2) _____

Ellie: Yes! Your turn.

Max: OK. This person lives at 45 Main Street.

Ellie: Hmm. I know that address. That's your house!

Max: What does this person do?

Ellie: Is it your mom? She's a (3) _____

Max: No! My dad's a postal worker! My mom's a (4) _____

Ellie: You win!

Get Ready to Speak

SPEAKING GOAL: Describe a Place
You can describe a country, city, or building. Describe where it is and how it looks.

A Read and listen to the description. Underline the location words. 85

> **Speaking Tip**
> Words like *in*, *at*, and *on* are location words. Use location words to help you describe where something is.

The City Hospital

My mom is a nurse. She works at a hospital. The hospital is on Elm Street. It is a big place, and it has a lot of rooms. My mom works on the top floor of the building. She helps sick people.

B Look at **A**. How does the girl describe the hospital? Complete the diagram.

1. ___It's on Elm Street.___

2. _____

The City Hospital

3. _____

Speak

C Think about a place that you know. Where is it? What does it look like?
Complete the diagram.

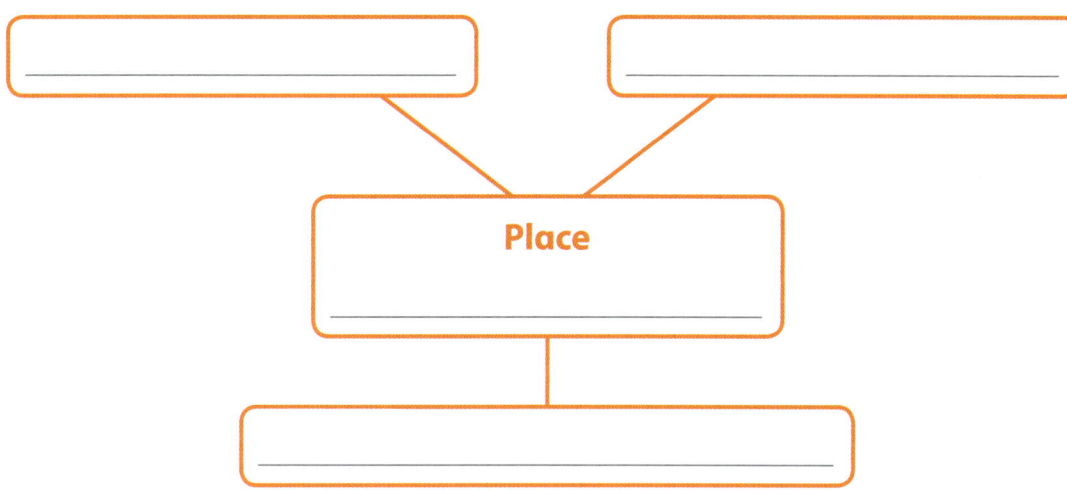

Place
_____

_____

_____

D Now write a description of your place. Use your ideas from **C**.
Choose new words, too. Then draw the place.

This is _____.

It is _____.

It is a _____.

It has _____.

 Ask your partner to tell you about his
or her place. Then tell your partner
about your place.

MY SPEAKING GOAL

☐ I can describe a place.

TOPIC

5

SOCIAL STUDIES

One Day Around the World

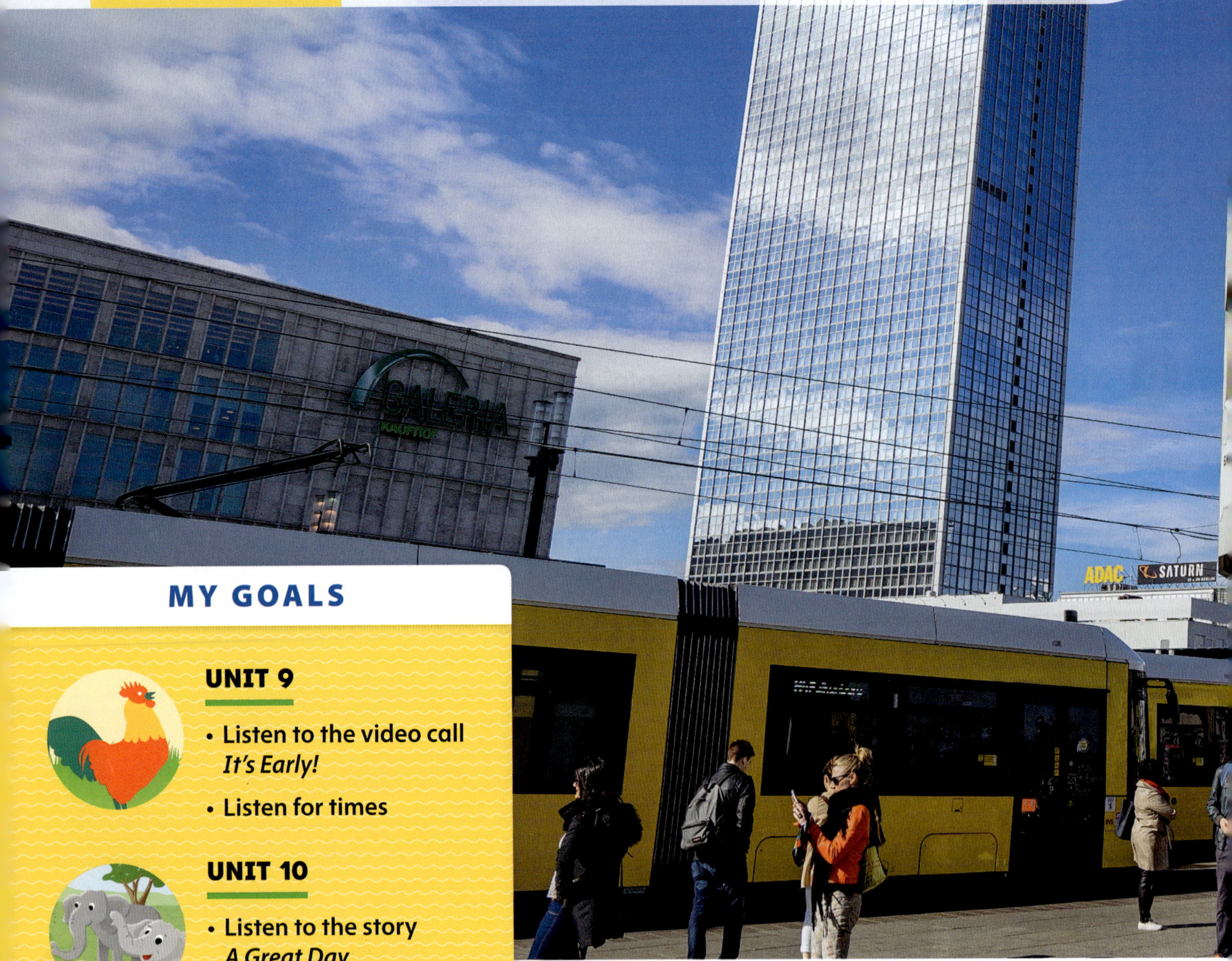

MY GOALS

UNIT 9

- **Listen to the video call *It's Early!***
- **Listen for times**

UNIT 10

- **Listen to the story *A Great Day***
- **Listen for sequence**

SPEAK

- **Make an appointment**

A **Look at the picture. What do you see?**

1. What can you see on the clock?
2. Do you have a big clock in your city? Where is it?

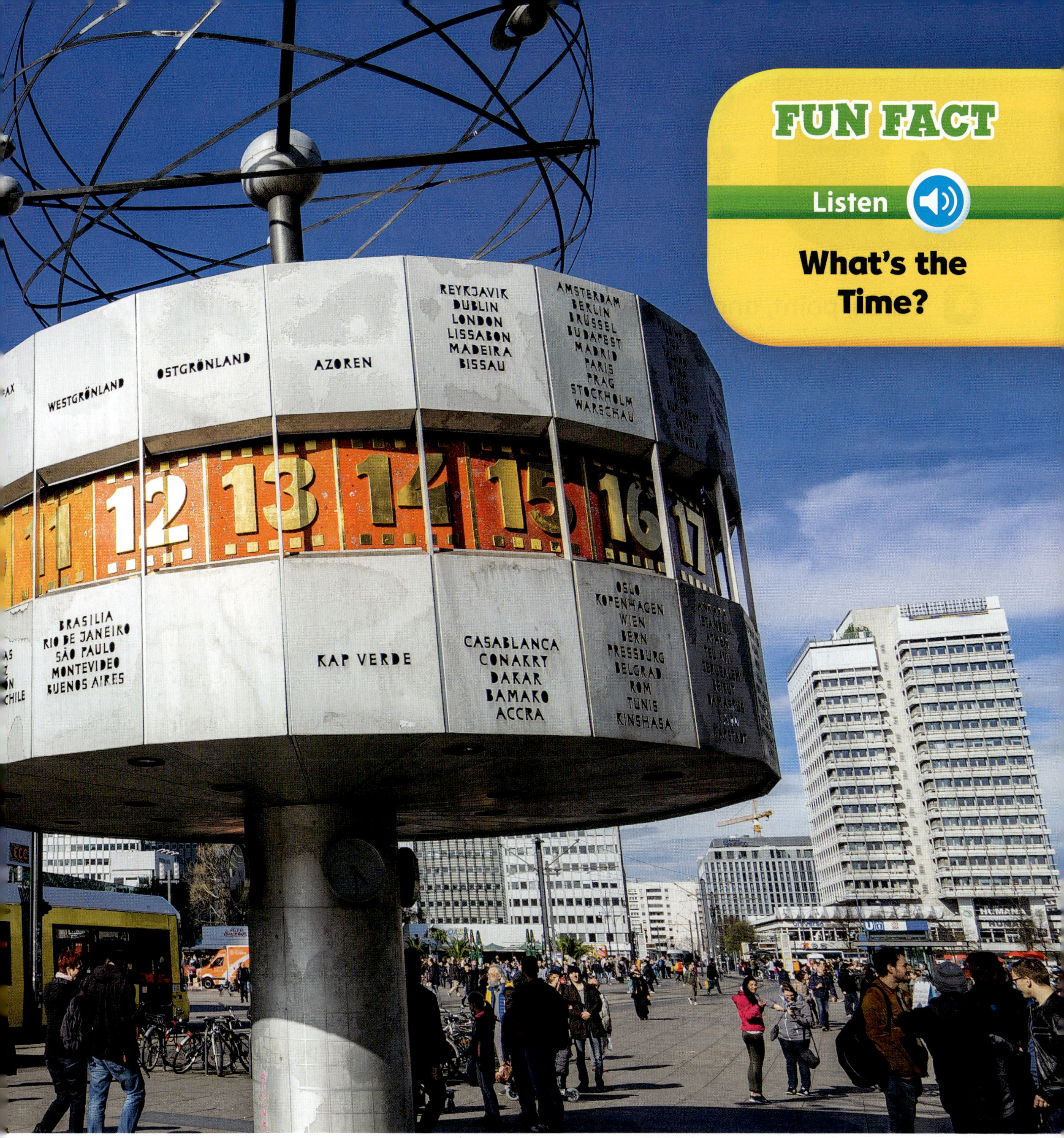

FUN FACT

Listen

What's the Time?

B **Listen to the Fun Fact. Then answer the questions.** 86

1. What does the World Clock show?
2. How do you check the time in places around the world?

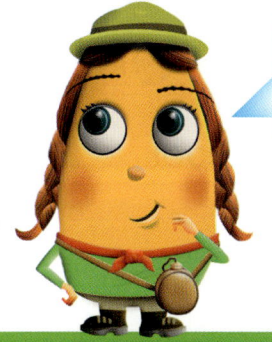

Think, Pair, Share
How do you tell the time?

Get Ready to Listen

Let's learn the **key words**.

A Listen, point, and say. Write the words in your picture dictionary. 87

get dressed

morning

walk to school

wash my face

B Listen and color. 88

C Listen and write. 89

1. __walk to school__   2. _____

3. _____   4. _____

Listen

A Listen. Then complete the sentences. 🔊 90

1. Kristi has math at _____9:00 a.m._____

2. Paul gets up at _____

3. Max eats dinner at _____

It's Early!

B Listen to the video call *It's Early!* What is it about? Choose the correct picture. 🔊 91

A

B

Now choose ✔ or ✘.

1. Yen and Li are in the same place.   ✔ ⊗

2. Li has English class at 3:30 p.m.   ✔ ✘

3. Yen washes his face and then gets dressed.   ✔ ✘

What do the **times** tell you?

Think! When do you talk to your friends on the computer or phone?

Understand

Remember!
Times tell you when
something happens.

A Think about **It's Early!** Read the sentences with times. Choose the correct sentences.

☐ a. It's 7:00 a.m. in England. It's 3:00 p.m. in Hong Kong.

☐ b. It's 6:30 p.m. in England. It's 2:30 a.m. in Hong Kong.

B Listen to **It's Early!** again. Choose the correct answer.  92

1. Yen and Li talk **at school** / **on a video call**.

2. Li is in **Hong Kong** / **England**.

3. In Hong Kong, the time is **7:00 a.m.** / **3:00 p.m.**

4. Li **has English class** / **talks to Yen** at 3:30 p.m.

5. Yen **gets dressed** / **walks to school** at 8:00 a.m.

C Listen. Complete each sentence with a key word. Then match. 93

1. It's ___morning___. It's time for breakfast.

2. I _____ at 6:30 in the morning.

3. She _____. Then, she goes to school.

4. The boys _____ at 8:00 a.m.

a. ____

b. __1__

c. ____

d. ____

D Listen to **It's Early!** again. Work with a partner. Complete the diagram with the correct times. 🔊 94

gets up	washes his face	gets dressed	walks to school
1. __6:30 a.m.__	2. _____	3. _____	4. _____

E Look at **D**. Write.

1.

He _____gets up_____
at 6:30 a.m.

2.

He _____
at 6:45 a.m.

3.

He _____
at 7:30 a.m.

4.

He _____
at 8:00 a.m.

MY LISTENING GOALS

☐ I can listen to the video call.

☐ I can listen for times to know when things happen.

Get Ready to Listen

Let's learn the **key words**.

A Listen, point, and say. Write the words in your picture dictionary.  95

afternoon

day

evening

sleep

B Listen and number. 96

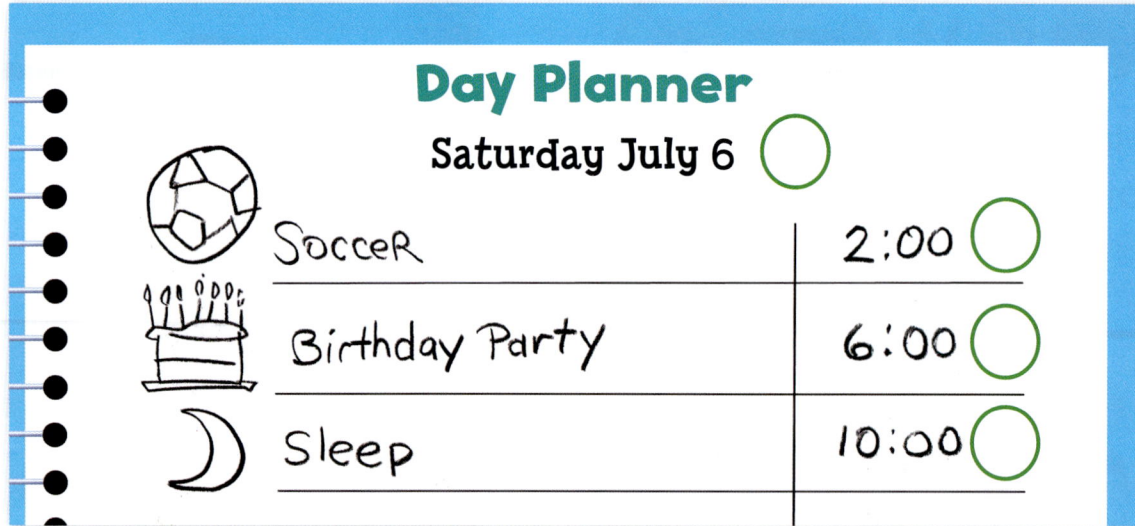

C Listen and complete the sentences. 97

1. Tim walks to school on sunny ____days.____

2. Liz watches TV in the _____

3. Yoko does homework in the _____

4. Kim goes to _____ late on Saturday.

Listen

LISTENING GOAL: Listen for Sequence

The sequence is the order things happen. Listen for words like *first*, *next*, *then*, and *finally* to understand the sequence.

A Listen. What happens first? Choose the correct answer. 98

1. ☑ a. Tim drinks water.   ☐ b. Tim eats breakfast.
2. ☐ a. Todd does his homework.   ☐ b. Todd goes to the market.
3. ☐ a. Sue talks with her friends. ☐ b. Sue watches TV.

A Great Day

B Listen to the story *A Great Day*. What is it about? Choose the correct picture. 99

A ☐

B ☐

Now put the sentences in order.

a. Pam talks to her mom.   ☐

b. Pam learns about animals.   1

c. Pam goes home.   ☐

Which words show the **sequence** of the day?

Think!
• Do you take school trips? Where do you go?

Understand

Remember!
Listen for **sequence** words. Words like *first*, *next*, *then*, and *finally* help you understand the order of things.

A Think about **A Great Day**.
Read the sentences. Choose **Yes** or **No**.

1. Pam has a soccer game. Then she eats lunch.   **Yes**   **No**
2. Pam has a soccer game. Then she walks home.   **Yes**   **No**

B Listen to **A Great Day** again. Choose the correct answer. 🔊 100

1. What does Pam do first on Friday afternoons?
   ☑ a. She eats lunch.   ☐ b. She has art class.
2. What does Pam do today?
   ☐ a. She has a soccer game.   ☐ b. She goes on a school trip.
3. What does Pam do on her school trip?
   ☐ a. She watches TV.   ☐ b. She learns about animals.

C Listen and choose the correct picture. Then write the key word. 🔊 101

1. ☐ a.   ☑ b.

___afternoon___

2. ☐ a.   ☐ b.

_____

3. ☐ a.   ☐ b.

_____

4. ☐ a.   ☐ b.

_____

D Listen to **A Great Day** again. What does Pam do on most Friday afternoons? Complete the diagram. 🔊 102

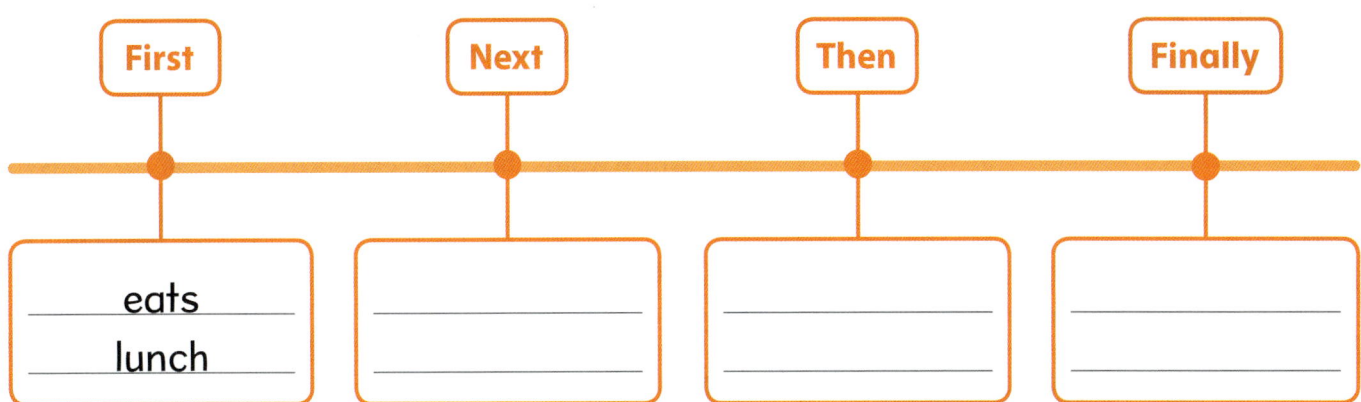

First	Next	Then	Finally
eats lunch			

E Look at **D**. Write. Use *First*, *Next*, *Then*, and *Finally*.

1.

First, she eats lunch.

2.

3.

4.

Remember!
Listen for **times**. What do they tell you? Listen for the **sequence**. Which words show the sequence?

A Listen to the story **It's Sunday!** What is it about? Choose the correct picture. 🔊 103

B Which sentences show times? Choose ✔ or ✘.

1. Jae gets up at 6:30 a.m. ✅ ✘
2. Jae eats breakfast in the morning. ✔ ✘
3. Jae walks to school at 8:00 a.m. ✔ ✘
4. Jae thinks it's a school day. ✔ ✘

C Which sentences show sequence? Choose ✔ or ✘.

1. Jae is tired. He wants to sleep. ✔
2. First, Jae gets up. ✔ ✘
3. Next, Jae gets dressed. ✔ ✘
4. Jae sees his friends at the park. ✔ ✘

D Listen to **It's Sunday!** again. Choose the correct answer. 🔊 104

1. What time does Jae get up?
   - ☐ a. 6:00 a.m.
   - ☑ b. 6:30 a.m.
   - ☐ c. 8:00 a.m.

2. What does Jae do after he eats breakfast?
   - ☐ a. walks to school
   - ☐ b. washes his face
   - ☐ c. gets dressed

3. What does Jae do at 8:00 a.m.?
   - ☐ a. talks to his mom
   - ☐ b. gets up
   - ☐ c. walks to school

4. Where does Jae see his friends?
   - ☐ a. at his house
   - ☐ b. at the park
   - ☐ c. at school

5. What happens at the end of the story?
   - ☐ a. Jae understands it's Sunday.
   - ☐ b. Jae has a fun day at school.
   - ☐ c. Jae plays with his friends.

E Listen to **It's Sunday!** again. Complete the sentences. 🔊 105

The clock rings. It's 6:30 a.m. Jae is tired. He wants to sleep. It's a school day. What does Jae do in the (1) __morning__ ? First, Jae gets up. Next, he (2) _____ and (3) _____. Then, he eats breakfast. "Hurry up, Jae! Don't be late," says Jae's mom. Jae (4) _____ at 8:00 a.m. He sees his friends at the park. Why aren't they at school? Oh, no! It's *not* a school day.

It's Sunday!

Get Ready to Speak

SPEAKING GOAL: Make an Appointment

An appointment is a plan to meet someone. An appointment has a time and a place.

A Read and listen to the appointment. Underline the time markers. 🔊 106

> **Speaking Tip**
> Use time markers, *a.m.* and *p.m.*, to tell someone when something happens.

A Doctor's Appointment

Liz: Hello? This is Doctor Park's office. Can I help you?

Eric: This is Eric Gilbert. I want to see the doctor. I feel sick. Can I make an appointment today?

Liz: There are two times open today, 10:00 a.m. or 4:30 p.m.

Eric: I can come at 4:30 p.m.

Liz: Great! See you at 4:30 p.m., Eric.

Eric: Thanks. Bye!

B Look at **A**. What do you know about Eric's appointment? Complete the table.

Appointment	
Person:	Doctor Park
Day:	
Time:	a.m. / p.m.
Reason:	

Speak

C Think about an appointment you want to make. Complete the table.

Appointment	
Person:	
Day:	
Time:	a.m. / p.m.
Reason:	

D Now write about your appointment. Use your ideas from **C**. Choose new words, too. Then draw the person you want to see.

I want to see _____.

Can I make an appointment on

_____?

I can come at _____ a.m. / p.m.

I want to see _____

because _____.

 Take turns making an appointment with your partner.

MY SPEAKING GOAL

☐ I can make an appointment.

It's Lunchtime

MY GOALS

UNIT 11

- Listen to the radio show *Kids Tell You How*
- Listen for requests

UNIT 12

- Listen to the story *Making Lunch*
- Listen for suggestions

SPEAK

- Give a food order

 A Look at the picture. What do you see?

1. What is the family doing?
2. Do you eat your food like this? When?

B **Listen to the Fun Fact. Then answer the questions.** 🔊 107

1. How old are chopsticks?

2. What are some chopsticks made from?

Think, Pair, Share
What food do you eat with a fork?
What food do you eat with your hands?

Get Ready to Listen

Let's learn the **key words**.

A Listen, point, and say. Write the words in your picture dictionary. 108

cabbage

chicken

onion

soup

B Listen and color. 🔊 109

C Listen and write. 🔊 110

1. _____ onion _____

2. _____

3. _____

4. _____

Listen

A **Listen. Then complete the sentences.** 🔊 111

1. The girl wants ___water.___

2. The boy asks for the _____

3. The girl asks to see the _____

Kids Tell You How

B **Listen to the radio show *Kids Tell You How*.
What is it about? Choose the correct picture.** 🔊 112

A

B

Now put the sentences in order.

a. Amy tells Jo how to make the soup. ☐

b. Jo tries the soup. ☐

c. Amy tells Jo what she is cooking. 1

What are the **requests**?

Think!
• What foods do you and your family cook?

Understand

A Think about **Kids Tell You How.**
What does Jo ask for?

☐ a. She asks for soup.

☐ b. She asks for water.

> **Remember!**
> Listen for *Can I* or *Can you*.
> We use *Can I* and *Can you*
> to **request** things.

B Listen to **Kids Tell You How** again. Choose the correct answer. 🔊 113

1. Amy is making **a salad** / (**soup**).

2. Amy's **mom** / **dad** makes this.

3. Amy **has** / **doesn't have** apples.

4. First, Amy cooks the chicken and **onions** / **rice**.

5. Amy cooks this for **12** / **20** minutes.

C Listen. Complete each sentence with a key word. Then match. 🔊 114

1. I like my Mom's ____soup____ on cold days.

2. There are red _____ on the burger.

3. I don't like _____ in my salad.

4. They eat _____ sandwiches for lunch.

a. ____

b. ____

c. __1__

d. ____

D Listen to **Kids Tell You How** again. What does Amy have for the soup? Complete the table. 🔊 115

	Amy has	Amy doesn't have
1. onion	✔	
2. cabbage		
3. apples		
4. chicken		

E Look at **D**. Write. Use *have* or *don't have*.

1.

I _____have_____ onions.

2.

I _____ cabbage.

3.

I _____ apples.

4.

I _____ chicken.

MY LISTENING GOALS

☐ I can listen to the radio show.

☐ I can listen for requests to understand what someone wants.

Get Ready to Listen

Let's learn the **key words**.

A **Listen, point, and say. Write the words in your picture dictionary.** 116

milk

potato

sausage

sweet corn

B **Listen and number.** 117

C **Listen and complete the sentences.** 118

1. My sister doesn't eat _sausages._

2. I have a _____ with my chicken.

3. Do you eat _____ for lunch?

4. _____ can help you sleep at night.

Listen

A suggestion is an idea about what to do. Listen for words like *Let's* to understand what someone wants to do.

A Listen. Choose ✔ or ✘. 🔊 119

1.

2.

3.

Making Lunch

B Listen to the story *Making Lunch*. What is it about? Choose the correct picture. 🔊 120

A

B

Now choose ✔ or ✘.

1. Beth and Theo are at school.

2. There are two people in the story.

3. Theo wants to cook food.

What is the main **suggestion**?

Think!
• What foods do you like? Why?

Understand

A Think about **Making Lunch**.
What does Beth suggest? Choose **Yes** or **No**.

1. Let's watch TV. **Yes No**
2. Let's make lunch. **Yes No**

B Listen to **Making Lunch** again. Choose the correct answer.  121

1. Where are Beth and Theo?
  ☐ a. at school   ☑ b. at home

2. What food does Beth ask Theo about first?
  ☐ a. potatoes   ☐ b. sausages

3. What does Theo want to drink?
  ☐ a. water   ☐ b. milk

C Listen and choose the correct picture. Then write the key word. 122

1.
  ☐ a.   ☑ b.

_____ sweet corn _____

2.
  ☐ a.   ☐ b.

3.
  ☐ a.   ☐ b.

4.
  ☐ a.   ☐ b.

_____   _____

D Listen to **Making Lunch** again. What does Theo want? Complete the diagram. Work with a partner. 🔊 123

```
                    ┌──────────┐
                    │   Theo   │
                    └──────────┘
         ┌───────────┘        └───────────┐
┌─────────────────────┐      ┌─────────────────────┐
│       wants         │      │    doesn't want     │
│ _____   │      │ _____ potatoes _____ │
│ _____   │      │ _____   │
│ _____   │      │ _____   │
└─────────────────────┘      └─────────────────────┘
```

E Look at **D**. Write. Use *wants* or *doesn't want*.

1.

   He _____ doesn't want _____

   potatoes. _____

2.

   He _____

   _____

3.

   He _____

   _____

4.

   He _____

   _____

MY LISTENING GOALS

☐ I can listen to the story.

☐ I can listen for suggestions to know what someone wants to do.

Listening Check

A Listen to the story **From the Farm**. What is it about? Choose the correct picture. 🔊 124

B What is the request? Choose ✔ or ✘.

1. We have cabbage.

2. Can I try the sweet corn?

3. Let's eat! ✔ ✘

4. We have onions. ✔ ✘

C What is the suggestion? Choose ✔ or ✘.

1. We have potatoes.

2. Our corn is great!

3. Can I try the sweet corn?

4. Let's eat! ✔ ✘

D Listen to **From the Farm** again. Choose the correct answer. 🔊 125

1. Where does Jill visit Zoe?

☐ a. at school ☑ b. at Zoe's house ☐ c. at Jill's house

2. Where does Zoe live?

☐ a. on a farm ☐ b. in a city ☐ c. near school

3. What does Zoe's family do?

☐ a. cut hair ☐ b. grow food ☐ c. paint houses

4. What does Jill ask Zoe?

☐ a. to try food ☐ b. to cook food ☐ c. to buy food

5. What does Zoe suggest?

☐ a. Let's cook food. ☐ b. Let's play a game. ☐ c. Let's eat the food.

E Listen to **From the Farm** again. Complete the sentences. 🔊 126

Jill goes on a trip. She visits her friend, Zoe.
Zoe is eight years old. She lives in a small
town. Zoe's family has a farm. They grow
food. "We have (1) __cabbage__ . We have
(2) _____. We have (3) _____.
And we have (4) _____," Zoe says.
"Can I try the sweet corn?" Jill asks Zoe.
"Yes, you can," Zoe says. "Our corn is great!
Let's eat!"
Zoe is very happy. She likes her farm.
Jill likes Zoe's farm, too.

Get Ready to Speak

SPEAKING GOAL: Give a Food Order

An order is a request for food in a restaurant or café. You tell your order to the server. Then, you eat!

A **Read and listen to the order. Underline** *please* **and** *thank you*. 127

> **Speaking Tip**
> Use words like *please* and *thank you* when you give a food order.

Today's Specials

Sue:	Can I take your order?
Eric:	I want the chicken soup, please.
Sue:	OK, great. Do you want anything else?
Eric:	Yes, I do. Can I have water, please?
Sue:	Sure. Thank you for your order.
Eric:	Thank you.

B **Look at** **A**. **What are the replies to the questions?**
Complete the diagram.

Question	Reply
1. Can I take your order? →	I want the chicken soup, please.
2. Do you want anything else? →	Yes, _____
3. Can I have water, please? →	_____. Thank you for your order.

Speak

C Think about food you want to eat in restaurant. Answer the questions. Complete the diagram.

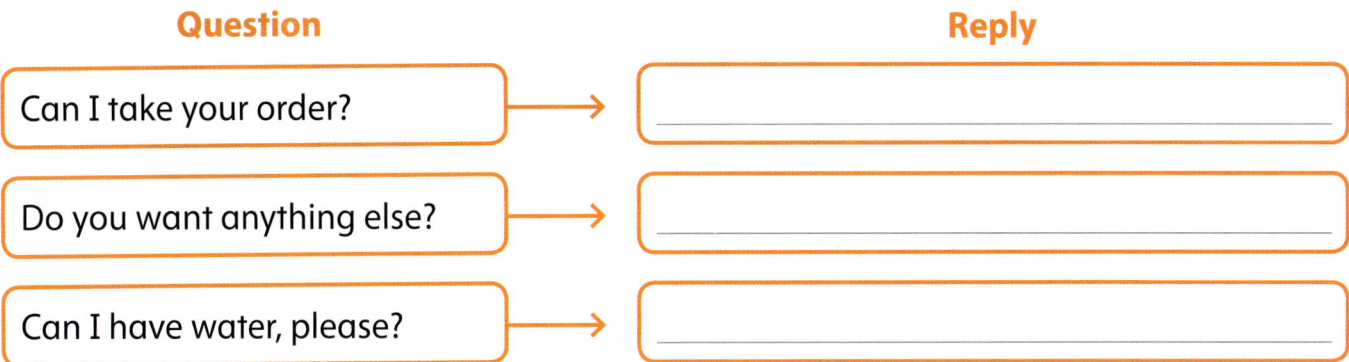

Question	Reply
Can I take your order?	→ _____
Do you want anything else?	→ _____
Can I have water, please?	→ _____

D Now write your order. Use your ideas from **C**. Choose new words, too. Then draw your food.

Today's Specials

_____

_____

Do you want anything else?

_____

_____

 What do you want to eat? Give and take a food order with your partner.

MY SPEAKING GOAL

☐ I can give and take a food order.

Listening 2
WITH Speaking

Workbook

Sarah Jane Lewis-Mantzaris

OXFORD
UNIVERSITY PRESS

Listen

LISTENING GOAL:
Listen for the Main Idea

Remember!
The **main idea** gives more information about the topic. It's in the first sentence.

A Listen to the passage **Friendly Faces**. Then put the pictures in order. 🔊 128

A

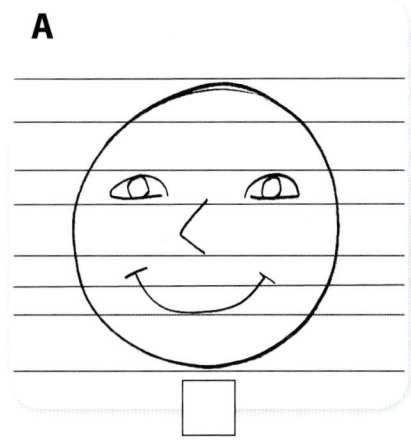

B

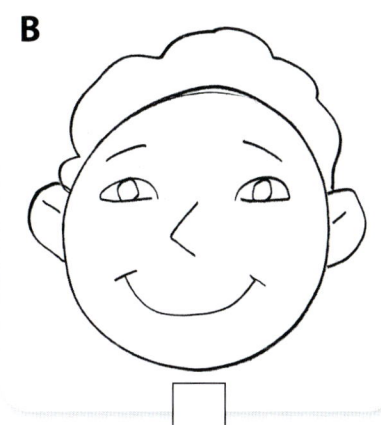

C

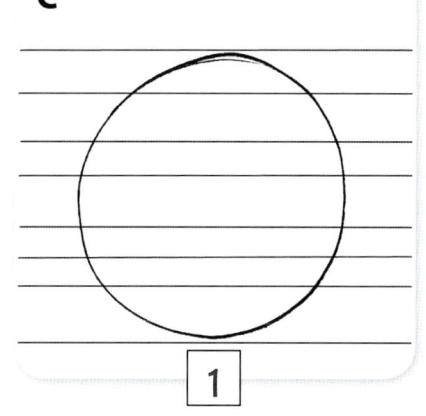

1

B Think about **Friendly Faces**. What is the main idea? Choose ✔ or ✘.

1. Making art at school   ✔ ✘

2. How to draw a face   ✔ ✘

3. How to draw with a pencil   ✔ ✘

C Listen to **Friendly Faces** again. Choose the correct answer. 🔊 129

1. What shape does she draw?
   ☐ a. a circle   ✔ b. an oval   ☐ c. a square

2. What do you use to draw the lines?
   ☐ a. a ruler   ☐ b. stickers   ☐ c. a crayon

3. What do you draw first?
   ☐ a. nose   ☐ b. eyes   ☐ c. mouth

4. What does the girl do last?
   ☐ a. draws Tom   ☐ b. draws the hair   ☐ c. colors the face

D Listen and write the word. Then choose the correct picture. 🔊 130

1. _____drawing_____

☐ a.   ✔ b.

2. _____

☐ a.   ☐ b.

3. _____

☐ a.   ☐ b.

4. _____

☐ a.   ☐ b.

E Complete the sentences.

| classmates | chairs | ~~decorations~~ | drawing | bookcase | stickers |

1. We are making _____decorations_____ for the party.

2. Eddie and Tina are _____

3. I'm putting the _____ on my book.

4. I use a pencil to make a _____

F Unscramble and write.

1. t s k i c e r

_____sticker_____

2. o e d c t r a s i o n

_____

3. l c a s m s a s t e

_____

4. a d r g w i n

_____

Listen

LISTENING GOAL:
Listen for Details

A Listen to the conversation **School Visit**. What do you hear about? Choose ✔ or ✗. 🔊 131

1.

a coat hook   ✔ ✗

2.

a poster   ✔ ✗

B Think about **School Visit**. What are the details? Choose ✔ or ✗.

1. Ada meets Noah's classmates.   ✔ ⊗

2. Ada visits Noah's classroom.   ✔ ✗

3. Noah shows Ada some drawings.   ✔ ✗

C Listen to **School Visit** again. Choose Yes or No. 🔊 132

1. Ada is Noah's sister.   (Yes)   No

2. Noah shows Ada his desk.   Yes   No

3. Noah's desk is next to the window.   Yes   No

4. Noah shows Ada a mouse named Fred.   Yes   No

5. There is a poster about turtles.   Yes   No

6. Ada goes to school next year.   Yes   No

D Listen. Then read and choose the correct answer. 🔊 133

1. What is by the classroom door?

a.  b. c. Planets

2. What is on the bookcase?

a.  b.  c.

3. What is Sue making?

a.  b. Bookworms c.

E Complete the missing words.

1. We put drawings on the wall of our _classroom._

2. I can find our country on the g_____

3. I hang my backpack on my c_____ h_____

4. My p_____ has pictures of turtles on it.

Speak

Remember!
A request is a question. You start a request with the word *can*.

Circle the word *can* in the sentences. Then think of your own requests. Tell your partner.

Can you pass me the stickers?

Can I have a pencil?

Listen

LISTENING GOAL:
Listen for Action Words

Remember!
Words like *run*, *jump*, and *swing* are **action words**. They tell you what people are doing in a story.

A Listen to the story **Don't Sleep!** Then put the pictures in order. 134

A

B

C

B Think about **Don't Sleep!** What sentences have action words? Choose or .

1. Rabbit can run.   ✓ ✗

2. Turtle is very slow.   ✓ ✗

3. Turtle can walk.   ✓ ✗

C Listen to **Don't Sleep!** again. Choose the correct answer. 135

1. Who is running a race?
   ☐ a. Rabbit and Cat   ✔ b. Rabbit and Turtle   ☐ c. Dog and Cat

2. What can't Turtle do?
   ☐ a. win   ☐ b. run   ☐ c. walk

3. What does Rabbit do?
   ☐ a. She walks.   ☐ b. She wins the race.   ☐ c. She sleeps.

4. What does Turtle do?
   ☐ a. He wins the race.   ☐ b. He runs.   ☐ c. He sleeps.

D Listen and write the word. Then choose the correct picture. 🔊 136

1. _____run_____

☑ a.   ☐ b.

2. _____

☐ a.   ☐ b.

3. _____

☐ a.   ☐ b.

4. _____

☐ a.   ☐ b.

E Complete the sentences.

| dance | ~~jump~~ | run | skip | swing | walk |

1. I like to _____jump_____ in the pool with my friends.

2. We _____ to our classroom at school. We don't run.

3. We _____ fast in the race. We don't walk.

4. The monkey likes to _____ from trees.

F Unscramble and write.

1. w s i g n

_____swing_____

2. k w a l

_____

3. p j u m

_____

4. r n u

_____

Listen

LISTENING GOAL:
Listen for Gist

A Listen to the passage **Bella Learns New Things**. What is the story about? Choose ✔ or ✘. 🔊 137

1.

Jo's friends   ✔ | ✘

2.

Jo's hobby   ✔ | ✘

B Think about **Bella Learns New Things**. What is the gist? Choose ✔ or ✘.

1. Jo has a dog as a pet.   ✔ | ⊗

2. Jo teaches her dog new things.   ✔ | ✘

3. Jo walks her dog every day.   ✔ | ✘

C Listen to **Bella Learns New Things** again. Choose **Yes** or **No**. 🔊 138

1. Bella is Jo's dog.   (Yes)   No

2. Bella can't hop.   Yes   No

3. Bella likes to dance.   Yes   No

4. Jo and Bella can't dance.   Yes   No

5. Bella can jump over Jo.   Yes   No

6. Bella is smart.   Yes   No

D Listen. Then read and choose the correct answer. 🔊 139

1. What can Carlos do?

   a.    b.    c.

2. What does Lucy like to do?

   a.    b.    c.

3. What can you do in the gym at school?

   a.   b.   c.

E Complete the missing words.

1. David can __run_____ fast.

2. My __h_____ is dancing.

3. I like playing __s_____ with my friends.

4. I can __h_____ on one foot.

> **Remember!**
> Use time phrases like *every Monday, Wednesday to Friday*, and *on the weekend* to show when.

Speak

Circle the time phrases in the sentences. Then think of other time phrases. Tell your partner.

I play soccer every Wednesday.

From Monday to Friday, I go to school.

I ride my bike on the weekend.

Listen

LISTENING GOAL:
Listen for Prices

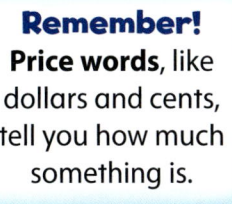

Remember!
Price words, like dollars and cents, tell you how much something is.

A Listen to the conversation **Cool Clothes**. What do you hear about? Choose ✔ or ✘. 🔊 140

1.

school

2.

shopping

B Think about **Cool Clothes**. Are the price words correct? Choose ✔ or ✘.

1. The T-shirt is 50 dollars.   ✔ ⊗

2. Lucy has 20 dollars.   ✔ ✘

3. Jill buys some clothes for 20 dollars.   ✔ ✘

C Listen to **Cool Clothes** again. Choose the correct answer. 🔊 141

1. Who do Jill and Lucy see at the mall?

   ☐ a. Jill's sister ☐ b. their friend ☑ c. an older girl

2. What does Mei have?

   ☐ a. a smartphone ☐ b. a watch ☐ c. some candy

3. What does Lucy want to buy?

   ☐ a. a T-shirt ☐ b. some candy ☐ c. a smartphone

4. What does Mei like?

   ☐ a. Lucy's watch ☐ b. Jill and Lucy's T-shirts

   ☐ c. Jill and Lucy's smartphones

D Listen and write the word. Then choose the correct picture. 🔊 142

1. _____smartphone_____

☐ a.   ✔ b.

2. _____

☐ a.   ☐ b.

3. _____

☐ a.   ☐ b.

4. _____

☐ a.   ☐ b.

E Complete the sentences.

| ~~clothes~~ | comic book | smartphone | T-shirt | vase | watch |

1. Your sister wears cool _____clothes._____
2. My friend and I put the flowers in a nice _____
3. I wear a _____ and jeans to school.
4. I call my mom on my _____

F Unscramble and write.

1. T - t h s i r

_____T-shirt_____

2. s v e a

_____

3. l c o t s h e

_____

4. m t a r p e s h o n

_____

Listen

LISTENING GOAL:
Listen for Days of the Week

Remember!
Days tell you when something happens. *Monday* is a day.

A Listen to the story **A Trip to Tokyo**. Then put the pictures in order. 143

B Think about **A Trip to Tokyo**. What days do you hear?
Choose ✔ or ✘.

1. It is Saturday today.   ✔ ✘

2. Phil goes home on Monday.   ✔ ✘

3. Yuto goes shopping on Wednesday. ✔ ✘

C Listen to **A Trip to Tokyo** again. Choose Yes or No. 144

1.	Phil lives in Tokyo.	Yes	(No)
2.	Phil and Yuto go to a mall.	Yes	No
3.	Phil is with his brother.	Yes	No
4.	Phil has 40 dollars.	Yes	No
5.	Phil's brother doesn't have a camera.	Yes	No
6.	Yuto and Phil look for some clothes.	Yes	No

1. What toy does Tom buy?

   (a.)    b.    c.

2. What does Kim have?

   a.    b.    c.

3. What do they put in the shopping cart?

   a.    b.    c.

E **Complete the missing words.**

1. There are many shopping carts   at the store.

2. I take pictures with my c

3. My younger brother has a lot of t

4. I like your toy p

Speak

Circle the phrase that exchanges information.
Then think of your own sentence. Tell your partner.

I like T-shirts. What about you?

My favorite store is the toy store. What is your favorite store?

Remember!
Use questions like
What about you? to
exchange information.

Listen

LISTENING GOAL:
Listen for Places

Remember!
A **place** tells you where people are. Places are countries, cities, and buildings.

A Listen to the conversation **My Favorite Job**. What do you hear about? Choose ✔ or ✘. 🔊 146

1.

a zookeeper ✔ ✘

2.

a nurse ✔ ✘

B Think about **My Favorite Job**. Are these places in the conversation? Choose ✔ or ✘.

1. restaurant ✔ ✘

2. New York City ✔ ✘

3. home ✔ ✘

C Listen to **My Favorite Job** again. Choose the correct answer. 🔊 147

1. What does May show Li?
   ✔ a. a picture ☐ b. a drawing ☐ c. a book

2. What doesn't Li like?
   ☐ a. restaurants ☐ b. cooking ☐ c. hot weather

3. Who is in Li's picture?
   ☐ a. a nurse ☐ b. a painter ☐ c. a zookeeper

4. What job do they choose for their project?
   ☐ a. a zookeeper ☐ b. a chef ☐ c. a barber

D Listen and write the word. Then choose the correct picture. 🔊 148

1. _____nurse_____

☐ a. ✔ b.

2. _____

☐ a. ☐ b.

3. _____

☐ a. ☐ b.

4. _____

☐ a. ☐ b.

E Complete the sentences.

| barber | ~~chef~~ | nurse | painter | server | zookeeper |

1. Dan is a _____chef_____. He cooks food in a restaurant.
2. The _____ works with animals.
3. A _____ helps sick people.
4. Colors are important for a _____

F Unscramble and write.

1. a i r n p t e

_____painter_____

2. f c h e

_____

3. z o e o k e r p e

_____

4. u n r e s

_____

Listen

LISTENING GOAL:
Listen for Addresses

Remember!
An **address** tells you where people live or work. An address has a number and street name.

A Listen to the story **The Wrong Address**. Then put the pictures in order. 🔊 149

A

B

C

B Think about **The Wrong Address**. What is the correct address? Choose ✔ or ✘.

1. The library is at 455 Park Street. ✔ ⊗

2. Mrs. Chen works at 455 Park Street. ✔ ✘

3. Mr. Lee works at 455 Park Street. ✔ ✘

C Listen to **The Wrong Address** again. Choose Yes or No. 🔊 150

1. The box is for Mrs. Chen. **Yes** (**No**)

2. Mrs. Chen is at the library. **Yes** **No**

3. Eli takes the box to the right address. **Yes** **No**

4. Mr. Lee is the librarian. **Yes** **No**

5. Mrs. Chen has Mr. Lee's box. **Yes** **No**

6. Mrs. Chen is Mr. Lee's sister. **Yes** **No**

D Listen. Then read and choose the correct answer. 🔊 151

1. Who helps Tom?

a. 　b. 　c.

2. Who puts things on tables?

a. 　b. 　c.

3. Who is working?

a. 　b. 　c.

E Complete the missing words.

1. The _barber_____ can cut my hair.

2. The p_____ w_____ puts mail in our mail box.

3. The s_____ works in the restaurant.

4. The l_____ reads books to us at school.

Speak

Remember!
Use location words like *in*, *at*, and *on* to help you describe where something is.

Circle *in*, *at*, or *on* and a place in each sentence.
Then think of your own sentence with *in*, *at*, or *on*.
Tell your partner.

The library is on Park Street.

My mom works at a small restaurant.

Listen

LISTENING GOAL:
Listen for Times

Remember!
Listen for **times**.
Times tell you when
things happen.

A Listen to the passage **Time for School**. What do you hear about?
Choose ✔ or ✗. 🔊 152

1.

a favorite sport ✔ ✗

2.

a walk to school ✔ ✗

B Think about **Time for School**. What sentences show times?
Choose ✔ or ✗.

1. Ali gets up at 6:00 a.m. ✓ ✗

2. Ali eats his breakfast. ✔ ✗

3. Ali walks to school at 8:00 a.m. ✔ ✗

C Listen to **Time for School** again. Choose the correct answer. 🔊 153

1. What does Ali do after he gets up in the morning?
   ✔ a. washes his face ☐ b. eats breakfast ☐ c. plays

2. What does Ali do at 8:00 a.m.?
   ☐ a. eats breakfast ☐ b. walks to school ☐ c. gets dressed

3. Who does Ali walk to school with?
   ☐ a. his brother ☐ b. his mom ☐ c. his friends

4. What does Ali cross on his way to school?
   ☐ a. water ☐ b. a park ☐ c. a road

Listen and write the word. Then choose the correct picture. 🔊 154

1. _____wash my face_____

☐ a.   ✔ b.

2. _____

☐ a.   ☐ b.

3. _____

☐ a.   ☐ b.

4. _____

☐ a.   ☐ b.

E **Complete the sentences.**

| do homework | ~~get dressed~~ | morning | walk to school | wash my face | watch TV |

1. I ____get dressed____ at 7:30 a.m. I wear jeans and a T-shirt.

2. I eat breakfast in the _____

3. I get up at 6:00 a.m. and _____ with water.

4. I _____ with my friends. I don't ride the bus.

F **Unscramble and write.**

1. w k a l   o t   c s h o l o

____walk to school____

2. s w h a   y m   c f a e

_____

3. o m r g n i n

_____

4. g t e   r d e s d s e

_____

Listen

LISTENING GOAL:
Listen for Sequence

Remember!
Listen to the **sequence words**. The sequence words tell you the order things happen.

A Listen to the story **It's Bedtime!** Then put the pictures in order. 🔊 155

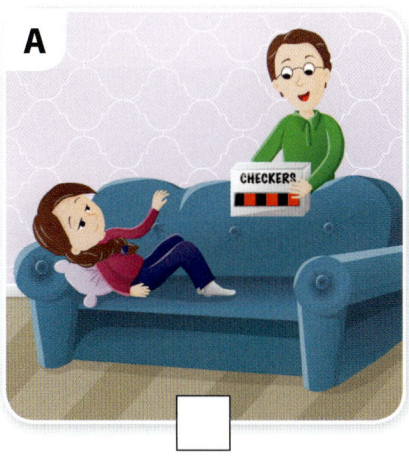

A

B

C

B Think about **It's Bedtime!** What sequence words are in the story? Choose ✔ or ✘.

1. First, Jill watches TV.   ✔ ✘

2. Jill reads her book.   ✔ ✘

3. Finally, Jill goes to sleep at 7:00 p.m.   ✔ ✘

C Listen to **It's Bedtime!** again. Choose **Yes** or **No**. 🔊 156

	Yes	No
1. Jill goes to bed early in the evening.	Yes	No
2. Jill watches TV and reads in the evening.	Yes	No
3. Jill is very sleepy at school the next day.	Yes	No
4. Jill and her dad play games in the afternoon.	Yes	No
5. Jill watches TV the next night.	Yes	No
6. Jill goes to sleep at 7:00 p.m. that night.	Yes	No

D Listen. Then read and choose the correct answer. 🔊 157

1. What does Tom do in the afternoon?

a.  b.  c.

2. When does Emily read with her mom?

a.  b.  c.

3. What does Sam do at 8:00 p.m.?

a.  b.  c.

E Complete the missing words.

1. I go to _sleep_____ at 9:00 p.m. on Saturdays.

2. We eat lunch at 1:00 in the a_____

3. I have a busy d_____ at school today.

4. My brother does his homework in the e_____

Speak

Remember!
Use time markers, like *a.m.* and *p.m.*, to tell someone when something happens.

Circle the time markers in the sentences. Then think of your own sentence with a time marker. Tell your partner.

My art class is at 11:00 a.m. on Tuesday.

I get up at 7:00 in the morning.

Listen

LISTENING GOAL:
Listen for Requests

Remember!
A **request** is asking for something. Use *Can I* and *Can you* to request things.

A Listen to the show **Onion Day**. What do you hear about? Choose ✔ or ✘. 🔊 158

1.

fruit   ✔   ✘

2.

a market   ✔   ✘

B Think about **Onion Day**. What is the request? Choose ✔ or ✘.

1. Do you like cabbage?   ✔   ⊗

2. Can I try this onion soup, Chef?   ✔   ✘

3. The onion soup is great!   ✔   ✘

C Listen to **Onion Day** again. Choose the correct answer. 🔊 159

1. Where is Mia?
   ✔ a. at a market   ☐ b. at school   ☐ c. at a restaurant

2. Who does Mia talk to?
   ☐ a. her friend   ☐ b. a barber   ☐ c. a chef

3. What is the main food Mia talks about?
   ☐ a. cheese   ☐ b. soup   ☐ c. pizza

4. What food does Mia eat?
   ☐ a. sweet corn   ☐ b. pizza   ☐ c. onion soup

D Listen and write the word. Then choose the correct picture. 🔊 160

1. _____ soup _____

☑ a.   ☐ b.

2. _____

☐ a.   ☐ b.

3. _____

☐ a.   ☐ b.

4. _____

☐ a.   ☐ b.

E Complete the sentences.

| ~~cabbage~~   chicken   pizza   onions   salad   soup |

1. Ryoko cuts some ___ cabbage ___ and onions for her salad.

2. You eat _____ with a spoon. You can't eat it with a fork!

3. These _____ have a bad smell.

4. I don't feel good, so I'm eating _____ soup.

F Unscramble and write.

1. n o o i n

_____ onion _____

2. b c a e b a g

_____

3. s p o u

_____

4. c i c n k e h

_____

Listen

LISTENING GOAL:
Listen for Suggestions

Remember!
Listen for **suggestions**
with *Let's* to understand
what someone wants
to do.

A Listen to the story **New Food**. Then put the pictures in order. 🔊 161

A

B

C

B Think about **New Food**. What is the suggestion? Choose ✔ or ✘.

1. Lee and Onur eat lunch. ✔ ⊗

2. Let's eat. ✔ ✘

3. Drink this water! ✔ ✘

C Listen to **New Food** again. Choose Yes or No. 162

1. Lee is at his friend's house. (Yes) No

2. Onur suggests they eat at a restaurant. Yes No

3. There is a lot of food on the table. Yes No

4. Lee thinks the sausage is hot. Yes No

5. Onur tells Lee to drink water. Yes No

6. Lee doesn't like the food at Onur's home. Yes No

D Listen. Then read and choose the correct answer. 🔊 163

1. What does Ruby want?

   a.    b.    c.

2. What does Anna eat for lunch?

   a.    b.    c.

3. What does Bill like on pizza?

   a.    b.    c.

E Complete the missing words.

1. My dad eats one _potato_____ every day.

2. I drink _m_____ for breakfast.

3. There is _s_____ _c_____ in the salad.

4. Mom cooks _s_____ and potatoes for lunch.

Speak

> **Remember!**
> Use words like *please*
> and *thank you* when you
> give a food order.

Circle *please* and *thank you* in the sentences.
Then think of your own sentences. Tell your partner.

Can I have milk, please?

Thank you, but I don't want potatoes.

Picture Dictionary

Write the key words.

Unit 1

_____

_____

_____

_____

Unit 2

_____

_____

_____

_____

Unit 3

_____

_____

_____

_____

Unit 4

_____

_____

_____

_____

Picture Dictionary

Unit 5

_____
_____

_____
_____

_____
_____

_____
_____

Unit 6

_____
_____

_____
_____

_____
_____

_____
_____

Unit 7

_____
_____

_____
_____

_____
_____

_____
_____

Unit 8

_____
_____

_____
_____

_____
_____

_____
_____

Unit 9

_____

_____

_____

_____

Unit 10

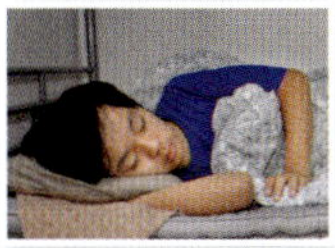

_____

_____

_____

_____

Unit 11

_____

_____

_____

_____

Unit 12

_____

_____

_____

_____

Syllabus

Topic	Unit	Listening Goal	Key Words	Speaking Goal
TOPIC 1 School Life	Unit 1	Listen for the main idea	*classmates, decorations, drawing, sticker*	Make requests
	Unit 2	Listen for details	*classroom, coat hook, globe, poster*	Focus: *Can* for requests
TOPIC 2 Games Are Fun!	Unit 3	Listen for action words	*jump, run, swing, walk*	Describe routines
	Unit 4	Listen for gist	*hobby, hop, rollerblade, sports*	Focus: Time phrases
TOPIC 3 It's Shopping Time!	Unit 5	Listen for prices	*clothes, smartphone, T-shirt, vase*	Exchange information
	Unit 6	Listen for days of the week	*camera, plane, shopping cart, toy*	Focus: Questions to get information
TOPIC 4 Where Do People Work?	Unit 7	Listen for places	*chef, nurse, painter, zookeeper*	Describe a place
	Unit 8	Listen for addresses	*barber, librarian, postal worker, server*	Focus: Location words
TOPIC 5 One Day Around the World	Unit 9	Listen for times	*get dressed, morning, walk to school, wash my face*	Make an appointment
	Unit 10	Listen for sequence	*afternoon, day, evening, sleep*	Focus: Time markers
TOPIC 6 It's Lunchtime	Unit 11	Listen for requests	*cabbage, chicken, onion, soup*	Give a food order
	Unit 12	Listen for suggestions	*milk, potato, sausage, sweet corn*	Focus: Use *please* and *thank you* for orders